TO THE READERS

Do you know what the strongest impression is of the clairvoyant, who reads the Book of Life? Yes, sometimes the abyss of world evil is revealed... At the same time however, it is shocking *how many great souls have been coming to the world!*

Plato, Cervantes, Shakespeare, Guillaume Belibaste, Haydn, Mozart, Ludwig of Bavaria, mother Euphrosinia, Seraphim the Tender... Many souls with the immaculate mark on their brow have been coming to the world and remain there in the subtle dimension forever. How many of them remain unknown as martyrs of Solovki or have been slandered after their death as Cathar Perfects... I experienced a great shock, when I saw the greatness of the many heroes, luminaries of love and kindness, who have been in the world. Let me call them to return for the final victory!

Our elder brothers and sisters are needed as never before. The descent of the souls with the immaculate mark on their brow and with the crown of the winner will predispose mankind to the decisive change towards good.

Day after day the world axis inclines more and more towards good. Who knows when the final turn will take place? Within one day or in a thousand years?

However, the time is coming when the world will become a million times kinder. Then golden rain will pour down from heaven! Every single drop is a priceless soul who has been on Earth before and now wants to come again for the final triumph of good, love, purity and peace.

Our Heavenly Mother, hear our prayer! Change the world, renew and purify it. You are the Queen of the world. You are the Mistress, and our All-Merciful Lady. Your reign and your power have come!

Everything that exists on Earth, our life and our breath are because of the Divine Mother. We are in inimitable debt to Her. She gives us everything and leads us on the earthly paths and will receive us one day into Her most radiant divine bosom.

Peace to you, I tenderly kiss your hearts and bless you not to leave the deck of our white otherworldly ship.

John Bogomil

N2'2016

CATHARISM

THE MAGAZINE OF THE INTERNATIONAL CATHAR MOVEMENT

WISDOM
LOVE
KINDNESS
PURITY
PEACE
MERCY
HARMONY
BEAUTY

JOHN BOGOMIL IS THE HERALD OF THE NEW EPOCH, THE APOSTLE AND THE PROPHET OF THE VERY QUEEN OF HEAVEN, WHO NOW ENTERS THE AGE OF HER GLORY. MORE THAN 500 BOOKS BY JOHN BOGOMIL ARE DEDICATED TO A VERY UNIQUE SPIRITUALITY, WHICH HAS NEVER EXISTED ON THE EARTH BEFORE. SEVENTY BOOKS OF THE REVELATIONS OF THE DIVINE MOTHER, WHICH HE HAS BEEN RECEIVING SINCE 1984, PRESENT THE PROPHETIC OUTLOOK OF THE DIVINE WISDOM ON THE MILLENNIUM TO COME.

The Divine Mother prophesies to John Bogomil about new and unique spiritual order of life. Her mission is to give birth to divinity within millions. The direct plans of kind providence include the building of a new human society – the Theocivilization III.

In accordance with the revelation of the Heavenly Queen, 83 previous civilizations died because of departure from the wise statutes of the Kind Universe and contemporary humanity is now entering into the 85th cycle. This crisis of the world will result in the birth of a new divine civilization by the mysterious participation of Divine Wisdom.

According to many prophecies and apocalyptic forecasts, the world now enters the final period of the last times. In the early 1960s in the Spanish village of Garabandal, the Most Holy Virgin revealed three warnings to humanity. The horrible tsunami in South-East Asia in 2004 was the first one.

Despite lots of signs and miracles, the Christian world conceals heavenly messages of the Divine Mother, which are given all around the earth. In Kibeho (Rwanda), Medjugorje (Bosnia and Herzegovina), Italy, Poland, America, Japan, Syria, Egypt – hundreds of apparitions and revelations, in which the Divine Mother reminds humanity about the tragic state of the earth and offers ways of rescue.

The Queen of Heaven names seven reasons for the possible destruction of the world:

1) Tibet, which secretly proclaimed itself to be the centre of the world governance.

2) Lower cosmos (astral world): forth dimension, astrology, contacts with UFO, cloning, test-tube conception etc.

3) World pharisaism and apostasy (degradation) of the churches.

4) Materialism: atheism, lack of spiritual life and the 'cult of flesh'.

5) Magic, which penetrated into all spheres of human activity.

6) Mammon: considering a human being just as a resource.

7) Dissolution of morals, outrageous debauchery and substitution of cultural and spiritual values. The obvious evil is posed as a virtue and a role model to follow...

Mankind should make a change, and return to the ideals which have been lost and start to draw from the source of true spiritual values. 'Three keys for salvation of the world are given, – states John Bogomil, – VIRGINITY, THE HOLY GRAIL AND SOLOVKI[1].'

Virginity – a new way of life without sin, which is possible through complete dedication to the Divine Mother.

The Holy Grail – a new nourishment from immaculate divine sources.

Solovki – the grace of martyrs of love, who through their suffering achieved the commence of the Divine Civilization on the earth.

Is mankind able to accept this message today?

The doors of the Ark are open. At its steering-wheel stands the great Admiraltess of divine humankind. In the apocalyptic desert of the modern world, She calls everybody to mount aboard of Her White Ship. ●

[1] Solovki – the name of the archipelago in the White Sea in the North of Russia. It was the spiritual capital of Hyperborea and ancient Rus. In the 1920's, it was the first concentration camp of the Gulag.

Photo: Gleb Nebov, 2015

Bogomil Divine Mother.
Modern icon by
Maria Leontieva

‘I LEAD HUMANITY OF EARTH THE SHORTEST WAY’

swan song, which distinctive feature is the *absence of evil*.

*

When Mozart heard an ominous theme in Beethoven's composition, he rebelled: 'there should be no darkness of this world in music! A tiny bit of shade could be: just two bars, no more! If three, this is already bad. *Heaven save us from a crescendo in the realm of evil!*'

The definition, given by Mozart to a musical genius: 'Love, love and love only!' is brilliant!

This world is a crescendo of evil. Mozart, in spite of being crucified by the villains, has always brought an ingenious *crescendo of good*.

I am learning from Mozart how to respond to the surrounding thick shroud of evil with love only; *to defeat* evil through *ignoring* it!

A VORTEX OF LISZTS AND WAGNERS

Mozart, Haydn and Beethoven were revolutionaries of the spirit; that is why Rome hated them and eventually submitted to their clandestine execution as the enemies of the Church.

This kind of inquisition within music continues to this day. Its target is not only living musical geniuses, but also music in general. Execution takes place at the spiritual or conceptual level.

The music theorist Adolf Marx, who lived after the Viennese classics, has founded a new pro-Roman school of harmony. Then came Hugo Riemann, who introduced a notion of 'Wagnerian endless melody' and began to reveal the 'romantics'. Then the concept of a 'symphonic style' appeared. Theodor Adorno finished 'the process' by creating the world rock culture.

EACH THEORIST, HAVING SUMMARIZED THE WORKS OF A PREDECESSOR, MULTIPLIED RATIONALISM IN MUSIC, WHAT IS EQUAL TO MULTIPLYING OF EVIL. THIS RESULTED IN DEGRADATION OF THE COMPOSING AND PERFORMING ARTS.

Atonality began not with Debussy or Ravel, but with Franz Liszt! In his last years of life, Liszt wrote very dark and demonic music, which was consciously atonal. It was Liszt, who introduced atonality into music!

A lot of composers were swallowed up into the vortex of liszts and wagners. Tchaikovsky managed to escape it miraculously and entered the national 'oasis'. The Russian genius was brought up at the Volga River in the Bogomil tradition, based on the archetype of Minne.

SIX-HUNDRED-YEAR-LONG YOKE OF ROMAN CENSORSHIP

Kindness is sinless. Kindness is a sign of holiness.

The news of the Romans is *evil*. It is not the Evangelium (Gospel; *ευαγγελιον*), but 'kakongelium' (from the Greek *κακός*, bad or evil), i.e. the *evil news*. Such institution is ominous...

Thought has been expelled from music by the Roman institution. According to the official religion, all thoughts have already been outlined with resolutions of the ecumenical councils. A person should only obey the conventional directive. If anyone has any ideas, he is a potential heretic!

One of the resolutions of the Council of Trent concerned *freethinking*. What was meant by this term? For example, if you will think of Christ freely, then for sure you will fall into one of 117 'heresies', such as Manichaeism, Docetism or Bogomilism...

Freethinking is the *ability to think* in a general meaning, and spiritually! But once man starts thinking, he is immediately labeled as a follower of one of the 'heresies': either it is Nestorianism, or the movement of the Albigenses or some other...

Inquisitors did not allow geniuses to be heard, marking them with the evil cliché: any thought in music means belonging to a sect!

Now it is clear why the world of music is in such a crisis today: the six-hundred-year-long yoke of Roman musical censorship!

Compassionate and peace-loving freethinking and entry into the depth of the conceptual archetypes are prohibited to the performers. The Inquisition is still deliberately dominating the music!

When musicians realize what happened, they will return to the true *freethinking*, i.e. they will understand that they are given the ability to *enter into a person's depth*, to penetrate his inner castles and to speak by playing the music of what is unspeakable.

It is possible, with the help of music, to resolve fundamental issues of existence, to teach a man how to conquer the fear of death, complexes and neuroses. That is what freedom of thought is required for!

*

The School-of-Liszt approach is a technical virtuosity without any content. Professors adhere generally accepted scholastic guidelines, and students and performers, members of an orchestra and conductors must adhere as well...

Musical education prohibits the spiritual growth of a musician!

DO NOT BE AFRAID OF FREETHINKING! A person thinks in concordance with the archetype, individually imprinted in his spiritual conscience. When he succeeds to find the truth of thinking freely, then he sounds great! When he touches eternal archetypal depths, he becomes immortal.

*

The musical geniuses were interested in Christ, however, they considered Him separately from the church, as a universal phenomenon. If even they used the Gospel plots, they did not do it at the demand of cardinals, but did it like Haydn, who composed

'YOUR MUSIC GIVES THE

The rehabilitation centre 'Egaztienea' (transl. as 'Bird Paradise') for children with intellectual development problems is situated in the town of Logroño in Spain. There is a shelter for the horses that have served their time in a circus or at a hippodrome and were rescued by employees of the shelter from death in a slaughterhouse.

For several months Mozart's pieces interpreted by John Bogomil sounded non-stop in the centre. The divine vibrations of love and kindness heal those whom modern medicine cannot help!

The letter of the project manager, Naroa Pérez Sabando, to John Bogomil:

Father John, your music makes miracles!

You are personally present here with every horse and every child, and restore their hearing by reminding them that there are a loving Father and Mother, Who are ready to die for them a

E STRENGTH TO WIN!'

million times. You restore the memory of their earthly mission. Through voicing the language of superior celestial spheres, you transmit love, purity and immaculacy, which are not of this world, to children and horses that listen to you with their open hearts.

The children, who previously could hardly coordinate their movements, are now doing the movement prayer, trying to copy you. Those who had problems with articulation and singing now sing the triumphal marches...

Your music gives them the power to win. Your love returns to them joy and the ability to listen to the Divine Mother; and not only to the children, but also to the horses that become kinder more and more.

READ THE REPORTAGE ABOUT MUSICAL MIRACLES IN LOGROÑO IN THE NEXT ISSUE OF THE JOURNAL!

his oratorio 'The Seven Cries of Christ' being blessed by the Order of Illuminati.

*

A common feature of all inquisitors is a complete lack of understanding of a creative work, as a result of contempt for people. Creative personalities, like Tolstoy or Tchaikovsky, have been their first enemies who have to be anathematized...

BOGOMILISM AND CATHARISM TREAT MAN IN A POSITIVE WAY (LIGHT-CENTRIC VISION) AND CONSIDER CREATIVE INSPIRATION AS AWAKENING OF THE DIVINE POTENTIAL. SIN-CENTRISM (SEEING SIN AND EVIL IN MANKIND) ON THE CONTRARY ELIMINATES CREATIVITY. ANY ASPIRATION TO FREE CREATIVITY IS IMMEDIATELY DECLARED A HERESY.

When the divine channel of spiritual and artistic creativity is sealed up, it leads to the 'creativity' of a different kind, i.e. dissolute and vicious.

*

HEARING THE NOTES WITH THE HEART

The main idea is paradoxical: SEEING THE NOTES, DO NOT SEE THEM. Not *to play* notes, but *to voice* them *from within*.

It is not enough just to see notes and play them on a string instrument or a keyboard. There should be no automatic process! *Having seen* a note, you must *hear* it first. If the stage of hearing is omitted, and the inner vibrational ear does not work, you will not touch the strings of the heart either.

A note is merely a symbol of music which resounds eternally! If you remember this, any instrument, from simple pipe to piano, becomes the Lyre of Orpheus.

Not only eyes and hands are needed to play music. It is rather more important to have a keen hearing, in order not just to hear (with hearing), but to *hear with the heart.*

The heart must be full of greatness of archetypal long notes, i.e. kindness, love and victory through *strastnoye* (dedicated suffering of the anointed soul).

THE REVELATION ABOUT THE WORLDS WITHOUT EVIL

Why have we been initiated into *intergalactic* kindness?

EARTHLY KINDNESS REMAINS WITHIN THE SHELL OF THE UNAMBIGUITY AND ONE-DIMENSIONALITY. IT IS IMPORTANT TO RECEIVE THE REVELATION ABOUT THE WORLDS WITHOUT EVIL, BECAUSE IT IS NOT ON THE AGENDA OF THE CURRENT CIVILIZATION.

We cannot imagine what good worlds exist! There are no parasites: flies, wasps or mosquitoes. Nobody toils and moils from 9 am to 6 pm. There are no polluting cars nor police nor prisons... There is no devil. So there is not even a pretext for evil!

However, do not think that dwellers of kind worlds twiddle their thumbs.

On the contrary, they are very busy! Being aware of evil that still exists in the Universe, they carry their crosses. Their souls are so noble and benevolent (*'bene'* means good), that they give their consent to suffer for others for the sake of the victory of good over world evil.

As in the 'mixed' civilizations good and evil coexist, so in the good ones evil is present partly, but only for the purpose of good defeating it through *strastnoye*! The music of Haydn, Mozart, Beethoven and Tchaikovsky is evidence that these worlds really exist.

*

It is a great honour *to play music-prayer for all humanity.*

How to explain to musicians that music is prayer, which has nothing to do with the prayer of religious pharisees? No one from the traditional religious institutes can pray at such an exalted level. It is impossible to pray to Jehovah this way.

Mozart's music is not for every day, for there is too much love in it. Beethoven brings oceans of love... All of Haydn is within one phrase from the interview to a British journalist, when Haydn was already over seventy: 'I am inspired solely by the existence of a *Kind God in heaven and kind providence on the earth*. When I think about this, I am so happy, that music is being born at once'.

It is brilliant! Haydn heard the Kind Dear God, whom we are revealing to the world!

*

As there are two kinds of theology: *scholastic* (Catechism) and *spiritual*, from elders, so the musical interpretation can be either scholastic (literal), or divinely inspired (from spiritual elderhood). We are speaking about the *elderhood's* piano school. •

CULTURE

GOD WANTS PEACE

Let mankind, which is tormented by wars, feuds and injustice, be assured that God is merciful and infinitely loves His creation. Moreover, the Most High wants us to become His instruments of divine love and mercy and not only in words, but having it witnessed practically and actively in our earthly service.

Love is a great art. Love excludes wars and longs for dialogue. Love presupposes mercy and sacrifice in freedom; a wish to give one's own life for one's brother, not to take his life, and a desire to serve God in the person of one's neighbour.

Peacemaking is the cross which requires maximum efforts and spiritual courage. True faith consists not only in following spiritual practices or dogmatic principles and liturgical statutes, but in striving for the ultimate goal of every religion, which is the unity between man and God and between human and human in divine love.

The conditions, necessary for preventing wars, are:
1. *peace between religions and denominations,*
2. repentance, and
3. the turning of mankind to the eternal divine values, named in the Gospel 'an imperishable treasure', which everyone should gather, according to Christ's spiritual commandment.

Revelation of the Divine Mother, September 19, 2001.

OF PEACE

CHARLES MERCIECA, PH.D.

CHARLES MERCIECA IS THE PRESIDENT OF THE INTERNATIONAL ASSOCIATION OF EDUCATORS FOR WORLD PEACE DEDICATED TO UNITED NATIONS GOALS OF PEACE EDUCATION, ENVIRONMENTAL PROTECTION, HUMAN RIGHTS & DISARMAMENT, PROFESSOR EMERITUS OF ALABAMA A&M UNIVERSITY

There are no human beings anywhere who may be considered to be identically the same. Even perfect identical twins, whose biological make-up is exactly the same, differ in some way or another in character and personality as well as in psychology and philosophy.

THE MEANING OF PEACE

In spite of such differences, human beings, from the beginning of times, have yearned desperately for one common element: peace. Every single person on earth, deep inside, would not trade peace for anything else. In spite of this reality, human history is characterized by one war after another. There is hardly one era of history, which was termed as peaceful.

Peace is described as a state of quiet and tranquility. It is viewed as freedom from war, cessation of hostilities, absence of strife, tranquility of mind, quiet of conscience. Peace in the community means harmony among diverse people. The question which needs to be raised here is this: If peace is something which everybody wants, how come no one seems to be able to get it, at least for an extended period of time?

The reply is simple. The seed of *peace is found in the heart of every individual human being*. In other words, peace develops from the inside of the human being.

IT IS NOT IMPOSED FROM THE OUTSIDE ON A PERSON OR A NATION. PEACE, BY ITS VERY NATURE, IS LINKED TO THE SPIRITUAL ASPECT OF THE HUMAN BEING AND NOT TO THE PHYSICAL SPHERE.

Also, peace is the source of happiness. Most people search for peace in the wrong places. They believe that wealth and money are sources of happiness that having a new car and an excellent house constitute a source of enjoyment, and that being a success in life, as revealed in one's popularity, contributes to serenity of life.

Unfortunately, such people all proved to be wrong.

If wealthy and successful people prove to be happy, it is because they have peace in their heart. This means that, although they value every material good they have, they are, by no means attached to it...

THE SECRET OF PEACE

Gautama Siddhartha who later became the famous Buddha of history, the greatest of the spiritual masters, who has been revered by millions of followers for some 2500 years, was born in a wealthy family. He had everything he wanted except for one thing: peace. To secure peace he gave everything he had to the poor and went out to lead a very simple life. He concentrated on the spiritual practice and serving.

Mahatma Gandhi, who virtually single handedly drove the mighty British out of India, discovered peace in his heart and brought it out of himself to share it with others very successfully. To this end, he elevated his spirituality to a higher level than that of the average person, through the practice of such virtues as humility, patience, meekness, persistence, and perseverance.

Christ stated that His purpose on Earth was to bring peace in the heart of everyone who was ready to accept it. He exhorted His disciples to give everything to the poor and to go and follow Him. By this He meant that we should not attach ourselves to the material things on earth to the extent that we value such earthly elements as more important than the spiritual sphere of life.

Peace is altruistic, which means that we must be concerned about the welfare of all people without exception. Such a concern will move us to do anything that is legitimate and appropriate to this end. In view of this, we may easily understand why governments throughout history did not succeed to bring about a permanent world peace. Governments, by their very nature, tend to be selfish and inconsiderate to the needs of others. In fact, we often hear government officials speak of American interests, Chinese interests, Russian interests, British interests, French interests and so on and so forth. Governments will become instruments of peace when they start viewing the whole world as one global family... when they start thinking world interests instead.

World peace could be achieved on a permanent basis if we keep in mind the words of former US President Dwight D. Eisenhower when he said in his farewell speech to the US Congress: *All people of all countries want peace, only their governments want war...* The reason lies in the fact that they do not seem to have a genuine concept of peace. They do not seem to realize that the greed for more and more of the material things of this world would end in destroying the happiness in our heart.

WAR PROMOTION BY BIG BUSINESS

“ WHAT I AM READING IN THE HEARTS OF EUROPEAN, AMERICAN OR RUSSIAN POLITICIANS IS NOTHING BUT EVIL, SELFISHNESS AND DARK INTENTIONS. THE BANK MAFIA IS THEIR GOD. EXPLOITATION OF SLAVE LABOUR AND SWINDLING THE NEIGHBOUR ARE THEIR IDEALS.

I HAVE NO ONE TO RELY ON, EXCEPT MY FAITHFUL ONES, WHO ARE ABLE TO REALIZE SOBERLY: PRAYER TO THE LIVING VIRGIN IS OF GREAT VALUE.

Revelation of the Divine Mother, March 6, 2014

In all industrial nations, big business controls the entire economy of the nation including the government. The ultimate objective of big business is the never-ending build-up of money and wealth. The concept of peace as a spiritual reality, as far as big business is concerned, does not exist, not even remotely. This explains why the great powers keep on pouring countless billions of dollars every year on weapons of destruction while, at the same time, they keep cutting down money from the social needs of the people, education, and health care.

This explains also why millions of people all over the world die every year from severe maladies. It is obvious that the governments are primarily concerned, not with the interests of their peoples, and far less with the interests of other nations, but with the interests of a small elite of big business headed by the weapon industry.

World peace is a human right that is sacrosanct and cannot be violated. We learn from history that when nations prepare for war, they all end up waging wars. At the same time, when nations prepare for peace, they all end up implementing peace.

POSITIVE AND CONSTRUCTIVE ACTIVITIES

THE CULTURE OF PEACE involves the promotion of constructive activities.

Since *peace is spiritual by nature*, we have to resort to the practice of virtue, such as:

(1) *courage* to do what needs to be done fearlessly in the best interest of everyone concerned,

(2) *wisdom* to select between alternative routes which lead to a genuine peace with ourselves and with others,

(3) *comprehension* of people's dire needs based on their sacrosanct right for decent life and survival,

(4) *fortitude* revealed in one's ability to encounter danger or to bear pain with coolness and determination,

(5) *counsel* which consists of our ability to give people the right advice which is altruistic and humanitarian,

(6) *knowledge* of moral righteousness which consists of justice in doing to others what we would have liked others to do to us, and

(7) *compassion* which enables us to undergo any kind of sacrifice to eliminate suffering from as many people as possible.

" MY CHILD! TODAY, I ADDRESS A REQUEST FOR PEACEMAKING TO THE WORLD. BECOME KINDER! LEAVE EVIL BEHIND AS AN IMPLEMENT OF REVENGE AND MEAN THOUGHTS. HATE EVIL IN THOUSANDS OF ITS MODIFICATIONS, AND PARTAKE FROM THE TREE OF GOOD, SO THAT I COULD NAME YOU MY CHILDREN AND BRING YOU TO THE BRIDAL SUPPER OF OUR BELOVED.

Revelation of the Divine Mother, February 8, 2012

EXPOSING THE ENEMIES OF PEACE CULTURE

The enemies of the culture of peace work silently seven days a week. They never stop to take a rest. Like devils, they seem to have phenomenal energy. These enemies constitute the evil of our society, which is basically composed of millions of good people who die every year miserably because their responsible government officials have constantly suffocated the culture of peace.

This may be due to the fact that the culture of peace is not very easily understood, since we have been all born and raised in a culture of war environment.

But the time is approaching when finally the culture of peace may be given a chance to work.

By exposing the enemies of the culture of peace, I do not mean to draw a list of people that would become our object of detestation. That would contradict the philosophy of the culture of peace, since we need to be tolerant but firm. We must be tolerant in accepting people's weaknesses and firm in not allowing such weaknesses mess up the lives of innocent people anywhere in the world. *We need to expose them in order to let them know that, regardless of the fact that they work silently, we know that they have established themselves as the mortal enemies of the masses of the population across every continent.*

Christ once said: *With prayer you can move the mountain.* And the Blessed Virgin Mary said in Medjugorje during the decade of the eighties to six children there: *With prayer you can suspend the laws of nature.* Mahatma Gandhi, a Hindu by religion, used the tremendous power of prayer, meditation and fasting to drive out successfully the British from India, in spite of their military might.

Through these spiritual devices, we are well equipped to bring about the collapse of the most lethal industry in the history of the world: the weapon industry.

" ONLY THOSE WILL BE NAMED MY CHILDREN, IN WHOM I CAN SEE MY ORIGIN OF INEFFABLE LOVE AND UNCOMPROMISING KINDNESS.

TRY TO GRASP THE LATTER CONCEPT. UNCOMPROMISING KINDNESS EXCLUDES WARS OR VIOLENCE, CONDEMNATION OR HATRED... MANKIND CAN BE HEALED ONLY BY AN INSTRUMENT OF PATIENCE AND WISDOM, LOVE AND KINDNESS. ADD THE INEVITABLE

EVER-VIRGINAL PURITY OF THE MOTHER-OF-PEARL-BONE, AND YOU WILL GET A PERFECT IMAGE OF AN ELDER. ALL OTHER METHODS OF DELIVERANCE OF THE WORLD FROM EVIL ARE FRUITLESS.

Revelation of the Divine Mother, February 8, 2012

Enemies of the culture of peace are characterized by negative energy. We need to counteract them by generating *positive energy*, which is more powerful than all the weapons they produce. Such a positive energy is bound to defeat the objective of their lethal product which is outrageous and inhumane.

A brief study of history reveals that each time people faced a problem and they united in the pursuit of good, they all generated good and positive energy to secure the kind of good they were after. So will it be this time again! •

MARVIN JOHNSON

A COVENANT OF SALVATION AND PEACE

The Divine Mother of Nightingale Mountain (a place near the city of Ephesus, Asia Minor, where the Mother of God spent the 15 last years of Her earthly life) tells John Bogomil about the end times of the earth. The Most Pure Virgin does not want to frighten Her children. However, today the danger of the end of life on Earth is as high as never before, and hardly avertable! Local wars shake nations and countries and do not develop into world nuclear war only by a miracle...

ONLY THE QUEEN OF HEAVEN has the power to forbid the omnicide of the earth in the atomic war nightmare.

The evil which dark forces bring under the guise of 'evolutionary good' is a grievous absurdity, a parasitic tumour on mankind's spiritual body. ONLY THE QUEEN OF HEAVEN can turn Earth's ship around in the direction of becoming a million-fold kinder just before a gathering disaster happens.

Only the Goddess Virgin Mother can transform our planet into a fragrant garden-city, inhabited by myriads of kind people, who live without any evil.

Personal and all-human salvation requires:

That we (1) accept the protection of the Divine Mother, the Queen of the Intergalactic Universe; (2) consider ourselves as Her sons/daughters on Earth and in eternity; (3) entrust ourselves to Her from now on and forever; (4) admit that She is the Mother of all kind worlds, nature, deities, and people, Who nourishes all with the same divine milk and Her blissful Revelation of the Word; (5) be assured that the earth is surrounded by a multitude of kind and friendly constellations and worlds, which are all united with the bonds of universal brotherhood.

The Divine Mother wants, through the mystery of virginal divine matrimony of Nightingale Mountain, to divinize humans and embody kind deities for their great mission on the earth.

The Heavenly Mother reveals the Father of a kind Universe, Who has nothing to do with evil, Who has no evil composition in Himself, Who does not bless evil and Who does not allow it in any way.

Christ, Muhammad, Mani, Buddha and thousands of kind anointed ones have been coming to the earth with the purpose to dispel the hypnosis of 'almighty punisher' ('God') and to open the *supreme love and kindness of our Father.* Their message was partly inverted to the opposite (otherwise, how could 'the Holy Inquisition' have appeared?)

The covenant with the Goddess-Mother is a covenant with the Kind Father against the 'almighty' imposter, who pulls the world towards the atomic apocalypse. The covenant with Her anointed ones, who carry authentic kindness, is also required. They have nothing in common with the mixed, good-evil demon, who pretends to be a god.

She is the Mother of Kind Providence, kind fate and kind destinies. A covenant with Her erases the fatal programmes of the soul, cuts all attachments and leads away from 'attractive' traps of the prince of darkness. She is the one, Who brings true salvation and peace.

Kind people, respond to the appeal of your Queen Lady Goddess Virgin Mother! Become Her sons and daughters right now, straight away! Take a pen and with admiration for the Heavenly Mother – as a sign of your covenant with Her! – put your signature here, on the white scroll, or on the tablet of your heart... Shed a hot tear as a sign of your gratitude to your Patroness-Mother. •

THE DESTINIES OF THE WORLD ARE IN THE HANDS OF YOUR SOLAR SOVEREIGN, WHOSE AUTHORITY OF MERCIFUL LOVE AND DIVINE-MOTHERLY KINDNESS EXTENDS BEYOND THE EARTH, TO THOUSANDS OF GOOD WORLDS.

I WILL INCULCATE AVERSION TO WAR IN THE HEARTS OF MILLIONS. WARMONGERS WILL SUDDENLY BE PARALYZED AND WILL NOT BE ABLE TO COMPLETE THEIR OMINOUS PLANS AND MOVES OF THEIR DEVILISH 'CHESS GAME', WHICH THEY PLAY WITH FLAGRANT THOUGHTLESSNESS.

THE DEVIL PREPARES REPARTITION OF THE WORLD. IN VAIN! ONCE AGAIN HE WILL ACKNOWLEDGE MY SOVEREIGN POWER AND THE MIGHT OF THE SCEPTRE OF THE MOST MERCIFUL PATRONESS-MOTHER OF MANKIND IN ITS MOST CRITICAL TIMES.

Revelation of the Divine Mother, March 6, 2014

A PRAYER TO THE QUEEN OF HEAVEN FOR THE SALVATION OF THE WORLD

To pray 150 times a day (three times by 50):

Rejoice, Patroness of the world,
against the third nuclear world war,
Blessed Virgin of Kind Providence,
Planter of Wisdom's garden of paradise,
Exposer of the pharisaic inhuman breed,
Unmask the sources of world evil and meanness!
Proclaim the start
of the civilization of pure love!

The One, who holds the threads of fates and destinies,
Sophia Pronoia of Kind Providence,
avert the global war, convert the world!
Expose the evil in its burrow,
which has prepared nuclear catastrophe for mankind.

The Cathar Divine Mother. A beadwork by Nikolina Kravchenko ►

VLADIMIR ALEYNIKOV is a living treasure of modern literature and an outstanding Russian poet. In 1965, together with Leonid Gubanov, he founded the famous literary fellowship called SMOG ('The Youngest Society of Geniuses') and has been its continuous leader. He is the author of numerous literary portraits.

Vladimir Aleynikov and John Bogomil are poets of the same generation, and almost age-mates. They are both innovators and avant-gardists, and yet, who have not lost the connection with classics. However, it is not the only feature which makes them related; but also persecutions against both of them, natural unworldliness and aspiration to the highest mysteries and ultimate issues of existence. Having just got acquainted, they immediately felt mutual closeness. Although they have not yet met in person, they carry on an endless brotherly dialogue.

Photo from the private archive of V. Aleynikov

THE MUSIC OF THE HEART

FROM THE BOOK 'POETRY OF REVELATIONS' (2013)

It is a well-known fact that books of John Bogomil are important to his contemporaries.

These books are a cure for many people, who live in our hard times.

They are healing and bring light.

They save. Precisely!

Let us now imagine the amazement and astonishment of our descendants, who will see and read (yet not fully comprehend) all writings of John Bogomil, the complete set of works: poetry, prose and diaries.

It is an entire library!

Large library. Huge!

Books from this library are to be read thoroughly and many times.

Comprehend and conceive.

It is all made by only one person, John Bogomil.

As for the so-called creative potential (however, it is better to call it more precisely – a gift)... Father John is extremely, I would say, limitlessly creatively gifted.

What courageous, resonant, triumphant and truthful freedom is in every verse!

What prolonged breathing which allows all necessary words to come up!

What mighty, irrepressible and fearless speech!

With all subtle lyricism which weaves through almost all verses of John Bogomil, the huge set of his poems and verses is an up-to-date and latest epos.

...Any verse you read sounds as a separate resonant melody.

And this melody becomes an essential part of the polyphonic sound of a poetic cycle or a book.

You can feel the breathing of a man, a creative breathing. It is the breathing of poetry. The breathing of an epos. The breathing of a spirit.

Every verse in any book of the poet is a convincing evidence of the revelation that John Bogomil experiences. He peers and penetrates into the existential issues of life and into such significant depths, which could only be expressed with the heartened, illuminative and accurate Word supported by the earthly tough experience, which was achieved through suffering of the poet.

John Bogomil is a born innovator in poetry. It is his natural gift and he is made this way.

He needs new ways of expression as the breath of life.

Why is that so?

Because being new is neccessary for comprehension of this world.

It is how Father John expresses his wonder at the world.

It is how he expresses every revelation he receives.

...An ardent, passionate *sermon* preached with inspiration drawn from heaven, revealed to the inner eye-sight; a serious, thorough and convincing treatise, well-reasoned and profound; a simple, sincere, cordial and inmost *friendly* letter; smooth, rather slowed-down and pure *elegiac melody*, filled with the vibration of all keen strings of the heart; the majestic and triumphant ode, charged with epic power; an accurate, strong, relevant, eloquent and photographically exact *characteristic feature*; a brave, short-spoken and accurate *maxim; a simple draft*, which seems to be unpretentious, but in fact turns out to be very substantial; ardent or wrathful, or strict, or joyful *interjections* (there are many of them of a various kind); *a sigh* of tiredness or relief, or appreciation; a moderate, noble *grief,* and uncontrollable, triumphant *joy*; an inmost, sacred *love,* and *hope*, so necessary for people; a faith as support from Heaven to Earth, and continuous foresight of new, inevitable *revelations* which swallow up darkness with marvellous divine light; *a riddle* as a ground for serious reflection, and *a mystery*, because it is impossible without it; childish *simplicity* or grown wise with experience; a ticklish *question* and sublime *naivety*, as represented in folk songs or tales; a candid unadorned *realism*, and a broad, world-wide *musical range*; and much more what you cannot even list here, constitute the poems of John Bogomil and make his poetry to be an extraordinary, exceptional, unprecedented and unique phenomenon of its kind.

...This poetry as a whole resolutely and stubbornly confronts destruction.

This poetry is the poetry of essential, victorious and triumphant creation.

...However, (I should mention this straight away) it is also phonetically rich and could be easily perceived orally, when someone reads it out loud.

It is more convincing evidence of a direct, important connection of this poetry with music.

What this music is?

(Eternal and incessant sound).

The music of the spheres?

(Voices and melodies which flow down to our ear from heaven).

The music of existence?

(Of every single year, day, hour and second).

The music of the soul?

(Inmost, desirable and quiet).

The music of the heart?

(Excited, candid and precious).

This is the music of creativity.

(Mysterious, sacred, which creates worlds).

John Bogomil works unceasingly with inspiration, from one book to the next, and tirelessly improves the light-keeping and light-giving, diverse world, which he has created.

He is the author of his own epos. •

THE PATH OF THE KNIGHT

POEMS FROM THE BOOK OF POETRY BY JOHN BOGOMIL
(literal translation from Russian)

ETERNAL MEMORY OF CATHAR PERFECTS

1 Give your protection, Oránta[25], to a flawless knight
Matteo Horán!

2 The rod of gradulation of the 21st century Cathars
is given to the immortal *Etienne Butarrá*!

3 Had long-suffering *Pierre Aró*
mounted the stake?

He defeated lust and evil of the world,
light and goodness multiplied above the globe.

4 Chaste *Jean Combél* from Lorca
wrung the neck of 12 mixed constellations
of the Zodiac.
12 'reptiles' lay at his feet obediently
at the centre of medieval Europe!

5 *Bernárd Guilhèm* went alone to fight against
thousands
and won over serpents in human guise –
a hundred-thousand-strong crowd of inquisitors
with the patronage of the Most Holy Virgin!

6 Glorious is the knight of Amor Fino *Bernárd Martín* –
an earthly stranger, a paladin,
a desposyn.

7 The knight of the Holy Grail Barbé Raymond
knows how to beat the red dragon.

8 *Pierre Dumás*, a Parfait, executed in April, 1240,
joined the assembly of minnesingers and minstrels.
He plays a shepherd's pipe every morning.

9 Blessed poetess, Perfect Mother *Marina*
joined, through her martyrdom, to the dynasty of
desposyni.
Now she mourns in the world wide grave-yard
during bitter prayer in the night.
Dedicates the earthly-born to the Queen
Mother-Virgin.
Blesses them with the immaculate conception.

10 Next to her is the Knight Templar *Raymond of Aguilérs*
victor over thousands of evil chimeras.

11 16 constellations of the kind Zodiac
greet the fearless knight, noble *Brézilhac.*
Any enemy attack will get stuck!

12 *Pons Capélle*, a knight from the town of Goía,
received a blissful rod from Sophia Pronoia.

13 Blessed marquise, Perfectess Gounód from Lanté
bashes out Haydn's wind andante...
And so forth and so bright
you may name them day and night.

14 Knights-lovers-of-good in the orbits of the Spiritual Sun
celebrate the triumph of the intergalactic revolution!
Evil is exposed as a miserable vanity,
shrinks as a sponge and becomes a nonentity.
Goodness prevails by millions of criteria.
Earth shines with the Sun of God-humanity!

25
Oranta is one of the names of the Divine Mother, which literally means 'The One who is praying for us'.

AT THE ROUND TABLE

Knights of the blessed Chalice sit at the Round Table.
Keep the Sword of Minne instead of a Kalashnikov rifle.
What brotherhood is among the faithful!
Without the slightest trace of corruption or filth.

Kind Mammy protects and they hold Her by the hand.
Sitting at the table they are blissfully content,
as if listening to the lullaby in the cradle.
A voluntary immigrant away from this world...

AT THE ROUND TABLE

Kindness will win one day for sure!!!
While evil, no matter how it hides itself,
loses the thousand-year-long battle.
Insanity of love is anything but a tragedy.
Do not seek the article about me in Wikipedia.

Earthly chronicles lie outright and blatantly,
being an enemy weapon against the Anointed one.

Searching for the truth is the main weapon against malice.
The Divine Mother defeats political technologies of riffraff,
which conceals behind mammon and governing authority
over private and state territory.

The territory of divinity is a human being.
Settle yourself. Keep the letters from your dear.

PARCIVAL'S QUEST FOR THE HOLY GRAIL

1 Parcival visits amazing elder Trevrizent -
the exstatic Consolament!
Exhortations come as from the horn of abundance.
Not a single question remains unanswered.
2 Before that was the obedience to the elder Gornemant –
scrolls of supreme wisdom came from above.

3 The weeping virgin Siguna was sitting on the tree –
playing the Lyre of Orpheus' strings.

4 In front of Montsalvat are impassable morasses.
The only way to come through it is to fly on the wings...

5 Spiteful scoundrels collect their trash –
got hit in the neck with the Chalice of the Grail.

6 Kind knights fight against evil spirits
for the project of God-mankind.
The air is clean and almost transparent.

7 The unquenchable candle is incomparable
to the kerosene lamp.
Knight, stock up with the ever-burning candle's light!

PSEUDO-KNIGHTHOOD

Lustre of the knight's sabre
and – as the Soviet Union state ensemble -
empty talks and lie,
like a cossack, stepping out of line.

Win over *yourself*, having spurred the horse of low passions.
And join the bird's singing orchestra.
Dissolve in the air as a flitting hummingbird,
as a tumble-weed. Until fears have hurt your brain.

Enjoy *inner* changes, but not outward,
do not lose, like a outcast, the last hope
to meet Lohengrin on a frail life-boat
far away, near an uninhabited island.

DECLARATION OF LOVE

1 I love you a million times more
than historical, institutional,
personified Chalice of the Grail.
Source of bliss from heavenly chambers.
Divinely seeing of the Father of Pure Love.

2 Your presence on Earth has multiplied,
Nourishing Good Mother, divinely kind.
Million-fold-kinder Sophia Pronoia.
The living sanctuary of unearthly peace.

I rave about *You*, live by *You* only and adore beyond measure.
Take *Your* protection against Lucifer's arrows.
Nothing exists which You cannot do.
Minne. Bonne. Amor Fino. Agape.

Appear. Become a million times dearer and closer.
Looking forward to seeing you in person.

IN THE CASTLE OF THE FISHER KING AMFORTAS

The Holy Grail appears
on San Salvador Verdadero
for its knights and faithful maidens.

Glorious are Lohengrins and Parcivals of the 21st century,
the Keepers of the Chalice of the Grail.

Has the castle of the Fisher King Amfortas
during night prayer been revealed?

Wonderful!

Splendid!

The amphora has been filled with myrrh within a few seconds.
In spite of being asleep for an entire millennium.

In the castle of the Fisher King Amfortas
The Mother of fifteen-hundred hypostases
carries the Holy Grail in Her arms.
Our beautiful Queen, the Kindest of the Kind.

CONSOLAMENTUM

1 Kind Father prescribed to his sons
Consolamentum, Bonamentum,
metanoia – Melioramentum.

2 Father, I have become slightly kinder -
an earthly dweller of heaven from Hyperborea –
and it made me live a million times better and sweeter.
The forehead is anointed with blissful oils.

3 Father, I have become slightly more philanthropic.
More intolerant towards evil, more patient while suffering.

4 The great solar Consolamentum
to earthborn potential deities and poets,
the consolation which mankind didn't know before,
deprived of the last hope.

5 But now it is given hope beyond measure.
Kind Father will help to expel Lucifer.

6 Mankind becomes kinder naturally.
Consolamentum! Consolamentum!

7 Exasperation leads to catastrophe and death,
regardless of the possible profits.

8 Kindness brings eternal life
for changing mankind.

9 To the sick, suffering, poor and destitute –
consolamentum, consolamentum!

10 Live for a thousand years and more.
To our kind Father – glory!!!

11 White navigators sail the luminous sea water-area.
Glory! Glory!

12 The virginal knight
helps to the inconsolable in hospitals.
Myrrhophoras are transferred
to the islands of the Blessed ones.

13 The healing components
of new spiritual composition are blissful.
Consolamentum. Melioramentum.

14 To our immortal, glorious
brothers and sisters –
Consolamentum. Bonamentum.

15 Become kinder and misfortunes will give up accordingly.
And the Mother of Fifteen-hundred hypostases will
console you.

16 Kind Father, pour consolation unto the Cemetery of
the Anointed ones of 1000 sq.km,
resurrecting Consolamentum!

AMFORTAS

You will not enter
the realm of the Holy Grail
without prayer,
like elder Amfortas,
who dies every single hour
for us.

The Holy Grail prolongs
the life of Amfortas.

The Keeper of the Grail
becomes a kind god with a cresola
postmortem,
that what he sees after has hardly
survived,
and has become the solar god-infant.

Having entrusted the Chalice to Parcival,
he gained the immortality in the castle of the Grail.

The Keeper of the Chalice becomes
the successor of the Christ's dynasty of Despósyni
and shares their Cross for Peace,
while suffering beyond the limit.

CATHARISM
Nº2 2016

THE MAGAZINE OF THE INTERNATIONAL CATHAR MOVEMENT

Published in English, Spanish, German, Croatian, Russian and Ukrainian

EDITORIAL STAFF

Authors: John Bogomil, Charles Mercieca, Brian Swansea, Sophia Deoro, Leonidas Lefko, Gilbert de Castro, Boris Plato, Polina Onipchuk, Lohengrin García de Yzaguirre, Petro Doroga, Jonathan White, Mario de Garcia, Victoria Bonmatí, Vladimir Aleynikov.

Editors and translators: Leonid Belov, Gleb Svetilnikov, Margaret Kearney, Minna de Groot, Myrrhophora Dennis, German Korneychuk, Borislav Martemianov, Lohengrin García de Yzaguirre, Sviatopolk Bulgakov, Klara Mikhailova, Valentina Markicheva, Ekaterina Tsyriulina, Mirofora Bondarenko, Alexandra Bezuglaya

Designers: Melchizedek Solntsev, Alexandra Latysheva, Anna María Alekséyeva, Bonita Klarich

Photographs: Gleb Nebov, Makariy Parfionov

PUBLISHER

The Cathar Temple
Glastonbury, United Kingdom
Web: www.cathartemple.org
E-mail: cathartemple@gmail.com
Telephone: +44 (0) 7466 825 441
+44 (0) 7746 277 614.

We invite brilliant authors, wise editors, talented artists, kind musicians, and merciful philanthropists to work together on books and journals of the Cathar Temple.

THE CATHAR TEMPLE

CONTACT DETAILS:

USA:
California +1 929 301 7316
www.cathar.org
cathars21@gmail.com

GREAT BRITAIN:
Glastonbury +44 7466 825 441
+44 7746 277 614
www.cathartemple.org
cathartemple@gmail.com

SPAIN:
Barcelona +34 636 409 594
asociacioncatarabarcelona@gmail.com
Valencia +34 960 644 649
asociacioncataravalencia@gmail.com
www.asociacioncatara.com
www.cataros.org

CROATIA:
Zagreb +385 (0) 95 893 04 53
Split +385 (0) 21 780 516
www.bogumili.org
bogomilus@gmail.com

BOOKS AND CDs OF THE CATHAR TEMPLE

THE FAMOUS EUROPEAN CATHAR MOVEMENT IS OF GREAT INTEREST TODAY AMONG A WIDE AUDIENCE RANGING FROM SCIENTISTS OF THE HISTORY OF RELIGION TO THOSE WHO ARE ENDEAVOURING TO SOLVE THEIR INNER PROBLEMS WITH SPIRITUALITY. WE CAN BOLDLY CALL CATHARISM A PHENOMENON OF HUMAN CIVILIZATION.

THE PARADOX IS THAT THERE IS PRACTICALLY NO OBJECTIVE INFORMATION ABOUT CATHARS. EVERYTHING THAT HAS COME TO LIGHT TODAY IS ORIGINALLY FROM INQUISITORS, THE DIRECT ENEMIES OF MEDIEVAL CATHARS.

THE MODERN CATHAR MOVEMENT LED BY JOHN BOGOMIL, A PROPHET, SPIRITUAL TEACHER AND WRITER, HAS LITERALLY RESTORED THE GREEN LAUREL OF CATHARISM BACK TO LIFE AGAIN.

IT IS QUITE LOGICAL TO SAY: IF YOU WANT TO KNOW MORE ABOUT CATHARS – ASK CATHARS THEMSELVES!

www.cathartemple.org

ISBN 978-0-9927011-7-8

978-0-9927011-7

Revelation of the Queen of Heaven to John Bogomil, 25.06.2015

John, I want to appear to the world in a new capacity which has never been revealed before, as the former capacity was only a prelude.

In front of me, there is A LARGE BOOK OF INTERGALACTIC DESTINIES, in which all are connected with each other. The time has come, My child! Its pages, blackened by complete darkness, are lightening noticeably. For My children, who revere Me on thousands of kind and mixed constellations, I can now painlessly reveal myself on Earth in thousands of solar hypostases, each one kinder and greater than the other.

MY GRACE WILL EMBRACE THE WHOLE HUMAN BEING

My child, the Bogomil Divine Mother exceeds all previous manifold images. I do not want you to represent Me one-dimensionally: Orthodox or Catholic Mother of God, Chinese Guan Min, Spanish Dama de Elche, Japanese Amaterasu... It was excellent that you could integrate My names, but now be prepared for My revelation of new solar images.

Former images such as Smolensk Hodegetria, Garabandal, Fatima, Grushev, and Moscow corresponded with *the black eon* with its obscure predictions, endless catastrophes and temporal victories of evil over good. The time of the agony of world evil has come and it is crucial to start to see things clearly.

Renounce yesterday's images of the Queen of Heaven, the one which has been in your habitual thinking.

My grace will embrace the whole human being with all his 144 inner constructions – altars, temples, decorated bedrooms, throne-rooms, shrines, fountains and beautiful architectural buildings, which will align with what I name as *the new sun of inner man.*

Our Kindest Father wants beauty and splendour of the Queen Lady Goddess Virgin Mother in one and a half thousand hypostases to exceed all images of outgoing civilizations, including intersections with the Jewish-Christian Mother of God and Christ of the Jerusalem period. The Byzantine image of the Mother of God does not have anything in common with the Jerusalem one. The deeper we look into the past, the more distant the original benchmark is – the opening star that will never set.

NEW GIFTS, NEW TIMES, THE NEW CHURCH, THE NEW DIVINE MOTHER

Heavens have so much to tell your poor planet, which is awakening from the seven-thousand-year sleep!

Listen attentively to the speech of cicadas and grasshoppers, nightingales and starlings, the chirr of dragonflies and singing of larks. Now imagine *the Acoustic Temple of the Word of our Kindest Father.* The Father of Heaven wants to tell you a million times more than can be told through human language or language of nature!

Become 'a tabula rasa' (a blank slate) forgetting about the recent past. If clichés weigh upon you, I will not be able to put the treasure destined for all humanity into your heart.

The complete set of My revelations in fifteen 1000-paged volumes is wonderful. However, for my precious children who are capable to hear and listen to what is unavailable for an unprepared ear, I have *new* gifts, *new* times, the *new* church, the *new* Divine Mother and *new* you.

THE OLD WAYS, ALONG WITH THEIR DELUSIONS AND HOPELESS TRAPS FOR MILLIONS OF PEOPLE, FALL INTO OBLIVION.

TODAY I AM THIRSTY TO PRESENT YOU WITH THE REVELATION OF LIGHT, WHICH MARKS A

NEW DAWN OF THE THOUSAND-YEAR GLORY OF OUR MOST HIGH.

The earth is awakening and the light of the New Sun reflects on it, the light of the Sun of the Divine Mother in Her fifteen hundred shining hypostases, one lighter, kinder and more beautiful than the other.

AMONG THOUSANDS OF WORLDS I HAVE CHOSEN EARTH

Earth will return to the Union of Kind Constellations only when My images, which mankind does not yet know but which are very well accepted on Big Bear or Berenice's Hair constellations, are revealed. Dwellers of the constellations of the White Bear and White Swan[2] send you heavenly barges filled with innumerable greetings, kisses and blissful gifts. Their white ships are full of delightful valuables and treasures directed to earthly brothers.

Choose *the dialogue with the Divine Mother* among an infinite set of alternatives!

The honour is yet to be given to hear the voice of the One, who simultaneously patronizes and leads myriads of kind constellations.

My child! I have chosen Earth among thousands of worlds. Do the same: choose the dialogue with the Divine Mother and complete dedication to Her from among infinite possible prospects and alternatives. *Only because of My patronage* Earth will get a radiant destiny predetermined for it since the beginning of time.

The consequences of boycott of My Revelation will be tragic and catastrophic. Humanoids get the unlimited power to continue the remodelling of Homo sapiens until it becomes a cheerless crawling reptile or a despicable buzzing dung-fly.

Remember: everything that humanoids and their henchmen from secret services say is a lie from A to Z! They know how to pull the wool over people's eyes and offer miserable pittances in the form of technocratic innovations... However, the consequences of the covenant with them are disastrous and fatal for mankind as a whole.

2
The Divine Mother names a few kind constellations. Read more about the Cathar Astrology in the article 'Gates to perception of heaven' on p.24 of the journal.

I HAVE CHOSEN PURE AND KIND PEOPLE

Worshipping the institutional Mother of God (be it Roman-Catholic or Byzantine-Orthodox) is hopelessly out of date. Let 'ufologists' not deceive themselves referring to the Old and New Testament, the 'Lives of the Fathers', and prophecies of elders...

I HAVE CHOSEN NEW MARTYRS, BOGOMILS AND EUROPEAN CATHARS, kind and pure people, who strive for perfection, divinization and bliss.

The world will be saved if it accepts the image of the Divine Mother as She is revealed by the Bogomils of the 21st century, otherwise it will die if mankind follows Tibetan UFO-centres or, what is even worse, humanoid prospects proclaimed in the meeting halls of the Pope, who is now rejecting My revelations.

I promise to give many signs of My permanent presence, in spite of abandonments and spiritual deserts, seeming defeats and fears which obsess modern mankind. Believe Me, you will receive the signs of My incomparably greater participation in your lives and presence within you than ever before!

Rejoice endlessly and let the blessed peace be in your hearts!

As *an Intergalactic Guide* I lead humanity of Earth the shortest way. Blessed are those who follow Me faultlessly and do not take a step back. I promise, eventually, the radiant destinies and endless joy of communication with the Queen of Heaven and Her retinue for My faithful children.

Peace be unto you! •

THE DRAMA OF ADAPTIVE REMODELLING

GODMAN VS DEMIURGE

Mankind is called to restore the archetype of the Seraphic godman within. Having been caught in a trap of the prince of this world, it has lost the solar light of the inner castles. Having agreed to pass Lucifer's 'modelling', it has lost the spiritual treasury.

Our inner castles used to be full of myrrhic fragrances, riches and countless gifts of Minne[3]. A sun was shining within all 144 inner castles, filling everything around, hearts, souls and all worlds with its light...

It is high time to get out from the abyss, which we, as divine souls, were pulled into.

UNMASKING THE SERPENT

The path of divnization starts with the realization of *adaptive remodelling* which all of us have passed. A godman was born to the earth in a forbidden way, 'from below' through adaptive remodelling. He endured 180 terrible neurosurgical operations in the astral womb of the lower cosmos. The most precious 15 of 100 particles of Minne, virginity and immaculacy, were taken away and were replaced with the alien substance of lust, mammon, rapacity, hostility, magic and fear.

The godman had never met evil before. Only when he came to Earth, he could realize the monstrous emptiness inside. The deep existential insight is needed into the fact that we were misled and deluded. That what was offered to us as gifts, advantages and good prospects, turned out to be vanity and spiritual theft!

The prince of this world promised to enrich us, but in fact, he deceived us, seized the gold and platinum of heavenly gifts which belonged to us and gave his lunar dust, rubbish and limber from astral dumps. Having realized the sacrilege which Demiurge committed to us, we present a claim to him indignantly, as to the lier, deceiver, and sly seducer and unmask him as a mean serpent.

3 Minne – divine, heavenly and virginal love.

SERPENT, YOU DECEIVED US!

YOU USED OUR INNOCENCE, OUR IGNORANCE ABOUT EVIL AND ARCHLY OUTRAGED US. WE REJECT ALL YOUR 'GIFTS' OF LUST, NASTY SODOMY, MAGIC AND WITCHCRAFT. WE SEND YOU BACK ALL MALICIOUS DAMNATIONS AND CURSES. WE DECLARE A SAVAGE WAR AGAINST YOU AND WILL FIGHT TILL FINAL VICTORY!

GET OUT! I REJECT YOU, PRINCE OF DARKNESS, AND RETURN TO YOU ALL POISONS, DAMNATIONS AND CORRUPTION. YOU HAVE NO POWER OVER ME! BEGONE!

The awakening of mankind from heavy sleep will begin after understanding the secret of adaptive remodelling. The first reaction of an awakened soul is tears: 'Oh my God, what have I done? Why did I agree that adaptive remodelling be carried out on me and embodied through the astral gates of the prince of this world? I have lost Your love, Your light, kindness, countless gifts and treasures. Instead, I got tins with rotten remains of lunar monsters... Forgive me, Father! Forgive me, kind Mother!'

We have to see clearly the conseqences of adaptive remodelling, realize the intensity of the damage and start the path of restoration of our divine being.

THE PATH OF BECOMING A SUN

Adaptive remodelling should be comprehended as *becoming lunar*. The prince of this world makes us become lunar instead of making us become a sun and 'grounds' us in the status of Adamites. The inner solar eclipse happened within us and the Sun of Minne went out.

The spiritual path starts with lighting up a candle of Minne. In spite of the heaviness of our sins, damages caused by the evil one, faults and falls, we are full of desire to overcome lunar darkness with the fire of Minne. Let us again and again inflame the candle of Minne! One day, it will flare up and become the Sun of Minne, which we have lost.

The main obstacle for *becoming a sun* is adherence to the old way of living of our 'old selves' (adamic part of our being). This way of living was imposed on us by the prince of darkness and mankind enslaved by him, remains in the hypnotic sleep of adamism. It is necessary to win over the order of this world, realize it as astral rubbish dump and be set free!

Minne implies a complete transformation of a person. He who follows the spiritual path of becoming a sun should permanently purify himself in the practice of catharsis, which in no circumstances should be reduced to confession, rituals and sacraments. Catharsis is a gift of illuminative perception of your spiritual heart. We descend into the depths of inner castles and expel bats, reptiles, scorpions, astral spiders, rats, and tarantulas from there and fill the spiritual heart with the light of pure love Minne.

THE FEAT AND EAGER PRACTICE OF BECOMING KINDER

The path of becoming kinder, which we follow heroically, should result with birth of the divinity inside of us. Human kindness is ambiguous and implies lustful 'warmth'. Within the order of this world, kindness is just the warmth of the family womb, which gives nothing but illusion of comfort.

Let us be born from above! Let us become vessels of our Heavenly Lady and accept from Her the fire of bliss of Minne, which will reveal the inexhaustible potential of a solar godman. Starting with a microscopic inner sun it will gradually become a fiery luminary until the whole human being will be embraced by the Sun of pure love Minne! •

THE PRIMARY SOURCE OF WORLD EVIL IS NOT THE FALL OF SOULS, BUT ADAPTIVE REMODELLING. What kind of dialogues take place when souls approach the earth during their embodiment? Why is a person incapable of getting rid of evil origins within? How to overcome the veil and revive the divine potential, which has been lost?

Read in the next issue of the Journal!

SOPHIA DEORO, LEONIDAS LEFKO

CIRCULATION OF THE SOLAR CHALICE

NIGHTINGALE MOUNTAIN – SOLOVKI – SAN SALVADOR VERDADERO

Two thousand years ago the Sun of Minne (heavenly love) shone over Israel, and for a short period of time, Jerusalem was graced with the ministry of Christ, the Hyberborean Melchizedek. However, although the ever-burning candle was not lit for long – the priceless treasure of the Holy Grail remained.

CHRIST HAS COME NOT AS A MISSIONARY OF JEHOVAH BUT AS HIS ADVERSARY! The great anointed one of the Father of Pure Love was inimical to the Second Temple in Jerusalem and unmasked priests as the offspring of the serpent who speculate upon truth. He was preaching with no fear whatsoever! He openly came to Jerusalem and converted thousands of followers.

People were amazed at Christ's coming to Israel. Ordinary Jews liked the universal truths revealed by Him. They recognized the shining messenger as the supreme Deity of the earth – the very Father of Pure Love, El-Elyon[4].

After having realized its defeat, the Sanhedrin became angry and planned revenge. For the first time, the teachings about the kind Deity and his philanthropic statutes were called blasphemy and heresy, worthy of execution without a court-approved sentence or a fabricated charge.

CHRIST TOUCHED THE ARCHETYPE OF ISRAEL. Its greatness does not relate to Rachel and Ezekiel's tombs, but to Pretoria's prison where Christ, the Hyperborean King of Minne, languished. Being honoured with the advent of the King of Kings, Israel has become a sacred place for the future divine civilization.

NIGHTINGALE MOUNTAIN: THE BRIDAL CHAMBER OF CHRIST AND MARY

Why did Christ stop His homily in Jerusalem? *Because here, the fullness of grace could not be poured; nobody was found deserving enough to say* 'yes' to the King of the anointed ones! A second period of annunciation was necessary – Nightingale Mountain, where Christ revealed Himself as the Bridegroom in white clothes.

Nightingale Mountain is a wonderful recrudescence of Hyperborea in the mixed eighty-fourth civilization (current ambiguous civilization). Here, close to the Greek Ephesus and Smyrna, the Mother of God was taken out of Jerusalem away from the Pharisees' pursuit. As Hyperborean spirituality was transmitted to Atlantis, so was the short three-year period of Christ's service in Jerusalem to the Bridal Chamber of Christ and Mary on

4
El Elyon – is the original name of the Father, which miraculously remained in the rewritten Bible where it is mentioned 4 times. In contrast to Jehovah, Adonai, etc., this name is the most ancient in origin and goes back to the worshipping of the Almighty Father.

Nightingale Mountain (sixteen years, till the blissful Assumption of the Most Holy Virgin, of bridal-chamber dialogue).

Then it was promised: 'The Gates of the Bridal Chamber are unsealed and they will not close again'.

Solovki's parousian Christ of the Second Coming came to Mary on Nightingale Mountain, and not Jerusalem! The King of the anointed revealed adequately for the first time and he was understood. Here Christ did not have to prove nor to prophesize... the Mother of God was for Christ as a God-Bride, and the pleroma, the fullness of divine love poured onto Her. That is why to know the Mother of God is to see Her as Minne...

THEOGAMIC[5] CHRISTIANITY OF NIGHTINGALE MOUNTAIN PROVIDED THE BASIS FOR SLAVIC BOGOMILISM AND CATHARISM. DURING THIS GREAT SIXTEEN-YEAR PERIOD THE GOSPEL OF THE MOST HOLY VIRGIN WAS REVEALED. THE ROSE OF THE SERAPHITES (BOOK OF REVELATIONS OF THE MOTHER OF GOD TO JOHN BOGOMIL) IS A MESSAGE ABOUT THEO-ANTHROPOGAMY (A MARRIAGE OF DEITY WITH MANKIND) AS MULTIPLICATION OF CHRIST IN LITTLE CHRIST-BRIDEGROOMS AND MULTIPLICATION OF THE DIVINE MOTHER IN DIVINE BRIDES.

Such is the mission of our Queen and Mother of Heaven: firstly, to return the children to their Father and then to make them Bridegrooms and Brides.

THE THEOGAMIC GRAIL OF SAINT ANDREW, THE APOSTLE, FOR THE SLAVS

On Nightingale Mountain the Mother of God gave the theogamic Grail to St. Andrew the First-Called (and later to St. John) and told him: 'Go to Holy Rus! You will be heard. Our message will be multiplied there. Those who partake of this Chalice, my son, will become Christs and Mothers of God. Blessed by the grace and fullness of the Holy Spirit, they will teach the great love and if someone deserves it – love completed *by marriage with Deity*'.

So in this way appeared SLAVIC BOGOMILISM: THE SPIRITUALITY OF THOSE WHO ACCEPTED THE MESSAGE OF NIGHTINGALE MOUNTAIN ABOUT VIRGINAL GOD-MARRIAGE AND THE MULTIPLYING DEITY: Christ multiplying in great and little Christs, and Mother of God in new Mothers of God.

Rus's spiritual atmosphere until baptism by Vladimir in 988 was filled with light, ineffable love and supreme Wisdom. Pantheons of kind deities with seals of Christ and Mother of God were spiritually present. Elders, during contemplating prayer, rose a few metres above the surface...

Thousands of new disciples of Christ practiced not only a religion but a *god-marital spirituality*. Listening to Apostle Andrew, Scythian elders easily renounced traditional, time-honoured conventions. Only love's criterion was taken into account. Scythian women followed the image of myrrhophores, and wanted to take the Mother of God as example, in whom they saw the embodied Slavic Goddess. And men became Christ's warriors clothing themselves in chastity.

A MYSTERY INSISTENTLY CONCEALED BY ROME: THE GENUINE MOTHER OF GOD OF NIGHTINGALE MOUNTAIN IS DIFFERENT FROM THE ROMAN MARY! THE GRACE OF THE BRIDAL CHAMBER OPPOSED BIBLICAL LAW. AMONG THE BELOVED, THERE CANNOT BE ANY LAW OR RITUAL RULES, AS IN THE OLD TESTAMENT, BUT ONLY TRUST, LOYALTY AND LOVE.

To Slavic people, Andrew and John heralded the Hyperborean Goddess in white clothes, the divine marriage and the triumph of divine love. They

5
Theogamy is marriage with Deity.

said that Christ and Mary were god-human, luminaries, not subjected to death. A genuine disciple of Christ and Mother of God is only he who desires to become a little Christ or Mother of God and accept the image and seals of *supreme kindness* from the theogamic Grail.

'BAPTISM' BY BLOODY VLADIMIR

The gloomy tenth century is Elohim's expansion of Byzantium. The Roman-Constantinople version of Christianity implied the worst features of Jehovah's worship. Christ was mixed with the evil old-testament god. The word about the Kind Father was erased and a violent evangelization of European peoples began – in essence converting them to the false Christianity of the prince of this world.

It is known that Vladimir's baptism was exceptionally violent (read the testimony of the Joachim Chronicle about Kiev and Novgorod Rus).

UNDER THE PRETENCE OF SPREADING THE 'TRUE FAITH', JOHN-ANDREW'S BRANCH OF CHRISTIANITY WAS DESTROYED.People were told that those who did not want to be baptized would be considered enemies of the prince ('if somebody will not come to the river tomorrow… let him be my enemy', Vladimir proclaims according to Nestor's Chronicle). Many Kievans found themselves in the Dnieper's water not of their own free will – 'not because of love but because of fear'[6]. Many people 'fled to fields and forests'.

A millennium of state-related Christianity in Rus caused the loss of the genuine Christ and Mother of God! Vladimir's Orthodoxy completely destroyed Slavic theogamism and forbade worshipping the Mother of God of Nightingale Mountain. It seemed that Bogomil spiritual Christianity was eradicated during the first years of 'Bloody' Vladimir's rule…

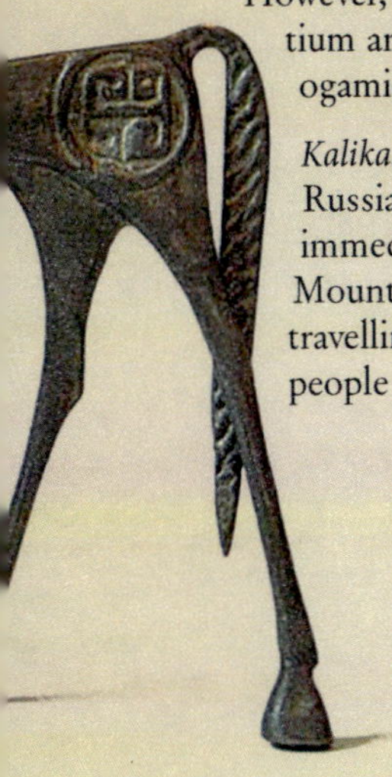

However, despite the excessive power of Byzantium and the genocide of kind people, theogamic Rus survived wonderfully!

Kalikas (wandering elders), familiar with Russian folk tales and spiritual poetry, were immediate heirs and apostles of Nightingale Mountain. *Kalikas* with wooden chalices in travelling bags brought spiritual revival to people and were turning them to divinization.

People were attracted by unworldliness, purity, holiness, and supreme wisdom of elders. *Kalikas* overcame evil by supreme wisdom and kindness. They took the vow of *supreme kindness.*

SOLOVKI BECAME A NEW NIGHTINGALE MOUNTAIN

By the eleventh century Christianity of Nightingale Mountain had spread to Rus and the Balkans, and was anathematized by Rome and Byzantium. Bogomils were exposed to genocide and underwent two exoduses: European (to the land of holy Catalonia) and to Solovki.

The Blessed Virgin herself took her people away from victimization. 'Go to faraway lands, – she told elders, – to lands which are paradisiacal and serene, blessed and divine, where our immaculate Hyperborean solar fathers lived. You will find peace, rest and beatitude there'.

Truly thousands of people migrated! From the first exodus of Slavic Bogomils to the Balkans and Pyrenees (in the 10-11th century) originated the Cathars, Templars, Dukhobors and Paulikians: the Great Church of Love. During the times of Vladimir-Suzdal's Rus (in the 12-14th centuries) in Moscow's princedom (and in the 15-17th centuries) the second exodus took place – to Solovki, where the Holy Virgin directly pointed.

Solovki's exodus was not inferior to the Jewish one. Until the 14th century a new Kitezh city shone in Solovki. These ancient Hyperborean islands became a new throne of the Bridal Chamber, a new Nightingale Mountain. The assumption grace of the Bridal Bed of the Mother of God came to Solovki in Russia. The Blessed Virgin was there. She was seen personally just like the theogamic Christ…

THE NAME 'SOLOVKI' [7] INDICATES THAT SOLOVKI MOUNTAIN IS DERIVED FROM NIGHTINGALE MOUNTAIN. SOLOVKI IS A RUSSIAN NIGHTINGALE MOUNTAIN, THE RUSSIAN BLESSED VIRGIN AND THE RUSSIAN CHRIST OF THE SECOND COMING!

6
In The Treatise on Law and Grace, metropolitan Illarion writes: 'There is no one opposing his pious behest, and whoever does it not with love but because of fear will be baptized, thus his orthodoxy is encountered with authority'.

7
'Of nightingales'

THE HYPERBOREAN CAPITAL OF THE HOLY GRAIL

It was hard to get to Solovki, since the 17th century Moscow tsars forbade visiting those sacred islands. They occupied the archipelago, and authorities turned it into a church prison... But those who passed through the gates of Solovki – entered the Hyperborean solar sphere, the Bridal Chamber of Nightingale Mountain, and went into absolute raptures and thrill over Christ's direct presence.

What did white elders teach about at Solovki? That the Grail brought to Rus by Andrew the First-Called is otherworldly. A vessel made of mother-of-pearl bone and parchment scrolls descended from kind divine civilizations and shone on Nightingale Mountain. Here, in the northern curved seashore, was the earthly capital of the highest immaculate galaxy of the Sun of Minne in zenith. One and a half million years ago the Chalice was brought there by celestials and it was called 'Holy Grail'. The Hyperborean capital became its first earthly throne.

Slavic Bogomilism and Catharism have the direct inheritance of the original Holy Grail. Access to the Chalice is only gained by he who is honoured with the anointment of Solovki, which is an entrance into the kind otherworld. (Paradoxically Solovki remained the Hyperborean capital in the eighty-fourth civilization!).

That's where pilgrims travelled! Not from England to India, not from Spain to Africa and back, but to 'the other end of the world', to the worlds of the 27th dimension. Through opened Solovki entrances they came to Hyperborea from where they were carried away to the Sun of Minne!

CATALONIA: THE CATHAR BOSOM

The Grail has the gift of miraculous multiplication. Remaining in the otherworld it appears at many different earthly thrones and everywhere it looks the same. No wonder that the Holy Chalice after the genocide of Slavic Bogomilism in the 10th century left for Solovki and at the same time was mysteriously brought to Catalonia through the Slavic countries of the Balkans, to the Cathar castle San Salvador Verdadero on a Pyrenean peak.

'Your presence in this country is not accidental, My child. I would call it by vocation equal to Holy Rus – Holy Catalan Spain, Catalonia of the future century.

Oh My Catalonia, My Cathar bosom! Oh the land I have chosen for the Second Coming, where every woody plant is fragrant with My glance and every iota of soil is blessed by My feet!'
(Christ to John Bogomil, 9.04.2006)

In value, San Salvador Verdadero is not less than Nightingale Mountain or Solovki. Moreover, this is the place where the name of our Almighty – FATHER OF PURE LOVE – was revealed. San Salvador is the mountain of His presence. From here His kingdom is spreading. Here is the place of His presence now and in days to come and forevermore.

The divine grace of Nightingale Mountain passed to San Salvador Verdadero. Christ and the Mother of God came here revealing the mysteries of the Bridal Chamber. The Grail awarded the dedicated with gradulational entrances to govern the world.

Byzantium and Rome pursued the Holy Grail. They needed the Chalice to implement a universal plan to take power. But there has never been an occasion when the holy vessel was at the mercy of the undignified.

A REMEMBRANCE LITURGY FOR 200 MILLION ANONYMOUS MARTYRS

It is difficult to understand the Holy Grail without Solovki and to understand Solovki without the Holy Grail. In the years of Gulag. it was mysteriously transferred to Solovki from the kind otherworld where blissful celebrations of the Chalice were held. The Holy Grail was carried to prisoners and then went to underground labyrinths...

Until now, the Holy Grail is stored in the territory of former Hyperborea, and as long as the shining Chalice is on the earth, the world will not perish and life on Earth will continue.

THE SOLOVKI LITURGY DOES NOT CEASE. IT IS CELEBRATED IN PRISONS, DISTRICTS, HOSPICES, HOSPITALS, AMONG THE PERSECUTED, UNEMPLOYED, HOMELESS, BEATEN UP BY RIOT POLICE… A LITURGY OF REMEMBRANCE FOR TWO HUNDRED MILLION ANONYMOUS MARTYRS – GREAT AND LITTLE CHRISTS, AS WELL AS MOTHERS OF GOD IN THE SOLOVKI DESERT.

Solovki is the world altar of the eighty-fourth civilization. It is an otherworldly archipelago that reveals the kind otherworld. The atmosphere of Solovki is divine, blissful and fragrant. It is the place of outrageous evil and boundless inhumanity, but at the same time of incredible love of the Divinity… Clothed with immortal spiritual bodies they descend nowadays from heaven - Polish, Georgian, Russian, Czech, German, American, French and Spaniards – all bring fragrances of Solovki and proclaim:

'The descendants of our divine grace will be protected and there will no longer be physical martyrs. It is enough that we suffered beyond the limits! But they will bear their crosses courageously as we have done it and they will deserve the brightest destinies'.

The Solovki branch is persecuted, driven out from the earth, but in the heavens, it will be glorified!

CATHARISM ORIGINATED FROM SOLOVKI

Do Bogomils take advantage before Cathars, Slavs before Europeans? It is a ridiculous contraposition. Do not try to understand the Cathar immortal ones in isolation from their origin!

The origins of Catharism lost in the 10th century are obviously not Western European. *Cathars are persecuted Bogomils who lost their Solovki fatherland.* Ten centuries ago our fathers emigrated from Rus to the Balkans and from there to Western Europe, where they found the *new* Solovki and new Nightingale Mountain.

Somewhere in eternity Solovki and Nightingale Mountain are interlocked, although it seems they have nothing in common. The archipelago of the White Sea, with ten months of darkness every year, ice, fog, bloody Sekirka[8] … – and the Bridal Chamber over the solar water area of the Mediterranean sea? But both Solovki and Nightingale Mountain in Russian have the root 'nightingale'. Here and there are Cathar ruiseñores[9], Bogomil nightingales.

THE ARCHITECTONICS OF MYSTICAL ENTRANCES

Just twenty kilometers away from Nightingale Mountain, in caves under Ephesus there is an entrance to Atlantis. There is also an entrance to Hyperborea on Solovki…

Why do we now speak about these ancient immaculate civilizations? Because these sacred sites are keys to help us to better understand the present day events that take place in these mystical spaces of the earth.

HYPERBOREAN SPIRITUALITY IS RETURNING TO EARTH, and its characteristic feature is *immaculacy*. The Mother of God revealing as the One-and-a-half-thousand hypostatic Woman Clothed with the Sun, heralds a new civilization which will be built by resurrected Hyperboreans and Atlanteans.

Some mysterious souls will descend on Earth. They will externally be as the common earthborn, but in reality, unprecedentedly new. They will uncompromisingly reject stamps of old religions, and old political systems. They will say: 'It is senseless to resort to old models, when the human is mixed with all kinds of evil. WE DESCENDED FROM HEAVEN TO INSTALL A DIVINE ORDER OF PURITY AND PROSPERITY'.

In order to open the gates for these wonderful souls it is enough to know the *architectonics of mystical entrances*: Solovki – Pyrenees – Hyperborea. •

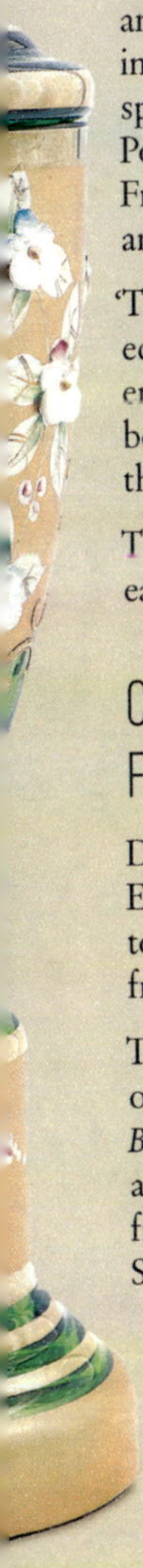

8 **Sekirka Mountain** is on the big Solovki island, where for many years, Gulag prisoners were executed by putting them into sacks and kicking them down a steep flight of stairs.

9 **Ruiseñor** means 'nightingale' in Spanish.

Mystical Neuschwanstein

JOHN BOGOMIL

O the perfect sanctuary of mysteries, Neuschwanstein!

THE MYSTERY OF NEUSCHWANSTEIN

KING AND KNIGHT LUDWIG II OF BAVARIA AND THE MYSTICAL ARCHITECTONICS OF THE CATHAR CASTLES.

LUDWIG II OF BAVARIA IS ONE OF THE TWELVE KINGS OF THE ATLANTEAN COUNCIL OF KINGS.
ON THE BANK OF THE DANUBE RIVER HIS GRANDFATHER BUILT A 'VALHALLA' – THE HALL OF FAME OF HEROES WHO DIED IN COMBAT. ON THE EARTH HIS GRANDSONS ARE DESTINED TO BE BURIED IN AN ANONYMOUS COMMON GRAVE, BUT IN HEAVEN THE ABODE OF OLYMPIAN DEITIES AWAITS THEM.
LUDWIG II OF BAVARIA BUILT HIS MEMORIAL OF THE HOLY GRAIL FOR ALL MANKIND IN COMMEMORATION OF ANONYMOUS HEROES, AND MARTYRS OF LOVE.

The castle of the White Swan... Nowadays, millions of tourists visit it without realizing the truth of where they have come... Today we will enter the *mystical Neuschwanstein.*

THE CHAMBER OF THE HOLY GRAIL

Two castles: Hohenschwangau of King Ludwig I and Neuschwanstein of Ludwig II were built from drawings which Bavarian king-knights had received from sacred Cathars and Templars. Both kings reconstructed and improved the Cathar castles after they were destroyed in the 13th century.

In ancient times the great Cathar castles related to the number of inner chambers of the god-man – 144 [10]. The Holy Grail (The Chalice of Christ's blood) travelled from castle to castle...

Cathar castles were unassailable fortresses. The legend about Montsegur ('there was a nine-month siege, then the knights surrendered and entered into the fire') is a Roman fairy-tale! The castle *withstood the siege for years.*

10
According to mystical Cathar teaching, there are 144 altars of the Holy Grail concealed in the human heart, which are a sealed micro space, a sacred universe of the Deity. When the inner temples are unsealed and awakened a god-man is born.

When the time came, the keepers disappeared with the Grail. This happened to four of the Montsegur parfaits: at the very last moment they escaped with the Chalice to a canyon...

Nowadays, alas! Nothing remains of the 144 castles except ruins. Rome always knew that if at least one castle were restored, Cathar spirituality would revive and shine, the very same spirituality with which the Roman Curia had been battling for many centuries!

If one were to try and reconstruct even one castle, then one would immediately face problems and prohibitions. The externally reconstructed Carcassone does not count. It is a Roman picturesque town with a cathedral decorated with malicious dogs...

STRUGGLE AND VICTORY OF THE GREATEST KNIGHTS OF THE HOLY GRAIL

Did anyone think about the cost of building the castle of Neuschwanstein? This castle was built by the greatest knight of the Holy Grail, member of the Round Table of the 19th century – Ludwig II of Bavaria.

By building a Cathar Castle against the will of Rome, Ludwig sacrificed his life. It was a brazen challenge to Rome and the Bavarian parliament[11].

His adored grandfather, Ludwig I had done the same with Hohenschwangau castle before him, at the beginning of the 19th century; it was specially built for his grandson's education. Having a strained relationship with his son (prince Maximilian and his wife were alien to his spirit), Ludwig I considered his grandson to be his successor, calling him king Arthur's ancestor. In Hohenschwangau the young prince was since childhood surrounded by the atmosphere of the Knights of the Round Table and the Holy Grail. He was obsessed with knighthood and subsequently reached the highest degrees of initiation.

Rome met the challenge and took revenge upon both martyrs of the Grail. The Bavarian kings (the grandfather and his grandson) were declared insane and they were dethroned. In 1886 Ludwig II was found dead in the bushes on the shore of the lake...

SPIRITUAL BEAUTY IS RELATED TO CONTEMPLATION OF DIVINE WORLDS

Answering his opponents who reproached him of waste, the king-knight said: *'I want to embody beauty'.*

He was not talking of aesthetic beauty but of *spiritual beauty in the Cathar sense*, crowning the *golden octonary* (supreme wisdom, love, kindness, purity, peace, mercy, harmony, beauty)! This beauty implies contemplating divine

11
The Bavarian parliament of two houses was since its foundation (1818) in a concordat (an official convention) with the Roman Curia. Parliamentarians hated both kings for 'waste' (they said that the kings squandered the treasury). It used to be said (not in public) that 'Ludwig II is the ancestor of the mad Ludwig I. He ought to be locked up, there is no other choice'...

worlds, the transition to the castles of Minne (heavenly love). The greatest crown on the earth is to achieve the beauty of parfaits.

The Cathar castles' architecture is not less mysterious than that of the Egyptian pyramids'. They have gates to the kind otherworld, to supreme kind worlds. Every castle had a geometrically and biometrically calculated hidden entrance. In the castle's underground there were secret caves and no stranger had access to them. On no occasion somebody unworthy could enter into them...

The surrounding landscape is marvellous and unusually beautiful! The Grail castle is always on the mountain (physical height presumes supreme spirituality), by the sea and surrounded by lakes. And the most important thing is that it is *a sacred place* identified by mysterious traits derived from Hyperborea.

SACRED CHAMBERS

Neuschwanstein is a masterpiece of Cathar spiritual architecture unequalled anywhere in the world. The castle architectonics are a mirror: its height is from twenty to forty meters, and as much in depth. The top floor is open to the sky. There are mysterious chambers in cellars where for decades and centuries Cathar knights, *parfaits,* dwelled. You have to know the password to open the door...

Behind the door there are ageless and young knights of the Round Table, favourites of both Ludwigs of Bavaria: Percival, Tristan, Sagramor, Gawain, Galahad and others...

VICTORS OVER WORLD EVIL

Knights not only visited Neuschwanstein but lived in its basements. When the time came they went out guided by the routes of the Chalice...

Others came through walls and others knew passwords and doors were opened for them. It is thought that only in the labyrinths of Neuschwanstein there have lived more than eighty knights of the holy Chalice. Having access to the first floors of the visible castle they directly participated in the sacraments of the Round Table and in their turn they brought Ludwig II of Bavaria into under-ground sanctuaries...

Knights who achieved victory over the vicious totality of world evil were called *victors.*

For each of the 1500 hypostases of divine kindness there is its caricature, a mask of worldly evil. It is necessary to attain the victory over all 1500 chimeras which are one way or another sealed in the inner in order to become *parfait,* perfect and crowned, and help others to win.

"Ludwig II of Bavaria", by Ferdinand von Piloty (1865)

Cathar castles
are earthly capitals of the Holy Grail and entrances into the Kind Otherworld

THE SPIRITUAL CAPITAL OF THE WORLD AND FORTRESS OF INTERGALACTIC SCALE

In cryptic storehouses of Neuschwanstein there are some *gradulational rods*[12] for ruling the world processes and one of the twelve chalices of the Grail. Sacred storehouses are called *gradulational chambers of the Bridal supper.*

PARFAITS **HAD ESOTERIC MAPS FROM ANCIENT ATLANTEAN TIMES HANDED OVER FROM CONSECRATED TO CONSECRATED. ON THE MAPS SACRED WORLD CAPITALS WERE PINPOINTED – PILLARS ON WHICH THE EARTH IS KEPT. NEUSCHWANSTEIN AND HOHENSCHWANGAU ARE AMONG THEM.**

12
The word **'gradulational'** – derives from 'gradula': a room in the highest tower of the castle from where parfaits ruled the world processes. The Catalan and Latin name of the Chalice 'Grada' originates from the word 'gradula'.

The story goes that AS LONG AS NEUSCHWANSTEIN IS THERE THE WORLD WILL BE PROTECTED FROM A GLOBAL CATASTROPHE. And the contrary: if the castle is destroyed there will be inescapable disasters and millions will suffer.

MUSICAL NEUSCHWANSTEIN

Haydn, Mozart and later Tchaikovsky, initiated into the mysteries of Swan Lake, in fact created music of the beautiful castles' architecture. Haydn's sonatas are a musical Neuschwanstein!

Goethe wrote a famous aphorism: 'Architecture is music carved in stone'. And here is... *music of Cathar castles' architecture.* Magnificent! The musical genius of Haydn, Mozart or Tchaikovsky cannot be expressed in words. But their divine musicological vibrations are embodied in the miraculous proportions of the Bavarian castle.

CATHAR JOY OVERWHELMED THE KNIGHTS OF THE HOLY GRAIL!

The greatest allegro, spiritual joy of the Round Table, is *a reward for the feat of renouncing evil,* when

a knight goes against worldly clichés and claims the victory. Spiritual joy shines on his brow and infects all by his example. The whole world begins to sing, dance in a circle, adore and hug each other!

Cathar joy fills the knights of the Holy Chalice in Neuschwanstein!

Joseph Haydn wrote about it in his diaries: 'I get up at five o'clock in the morning and kneel down praying to the Mother of God... *about the gift of joy!*

There is a lot of evil, grief, and anguish in the world! Joy is only available to some people. For thirty years I have led the orchestra in the castle of the Austro-Hungarian prince Esterhazy. And so what? The orchestra was supported by my energy! Musicians' faces are gloomy and dark till I share joy with them. Where does joy come from? Only from the Mother of God!'

Haydn spoke as a genuine Cathar. Only such joy consoles people! To tell stories about salvation, lift up the cup, give out indulgences or offer some other virtual keys are of little value. People need elation, divine spiritual light, which *cures and gives new birth.*

How can it be reached? *By achieving victory over personal evil and fatal programme.*

The primary consideration of a Cathar parfait (one who has reached spiritual perfection) and knight, is the absolute kindness and special enlightened joy of a man who has chosen to leave the circle of 'life-and-death', and who has entered the kingdom of divine love which offers victory over death. This is priceless!

THE ROMAN SYSTEM OF THREE FEARS

Alas! Most people are immersed in the order of dominant evil. They become gloomy, feel desperate, lonely and desolate... The spirit of this world casts a soul into a state of everlasting fear supported by religious institutions.

Religious fundamentalism needs an intensifying fear (fate, desperation): God is frightening, the soul must pass through the last judgment and more likely there will be a terrible fate in eternity...

In Catharism, the Roman system of three fears is completely overcome (frightening god, frightening judgment and destiny), The Father is loving and patient. Destinies are bright. Judgment in eternity is only a court made by our own conscience: man deserves what he has earned during his earthly life.

THE CASTLE OF THE WHITE SWAN

The spiritual sun has been shining over Cathar castles Neuschwanstein and Hohenschwangau constantly. The mysterious light did not die away miraculously and only became dim for some hours at night and at first light it kindled into a fiery disk...

The consecrated believed that each castle is a copy of one of the immaculate civilizations of the Intergalactic Ecumene, i.e. the sacrament of one of the sixteen kind constellations.

Built as a totality of all Cathar castles of the 12th-14th centuries, Neuschwanstein was called *the apotheosis of the Bridal Feast* and corresponded with the sign of the *White Swan.*

Knights worshipped this symbol. On clothes, and on holy banners, the White Swan was everywhere. Swan Lake derives its name from it... The White Swan is the victory over death by the force of supreme love.

THE SWAN SONG

The knights said: be prepared to leave this world in order to become *an apotheosis of Minne* – transition to the eternal reality of the Deity!

The transitional moment is the most difficult; it is an epitome of one's whole life. All worldly evil approaches the dying person! If the soul has been prepared it considers death as a consecration and *makes inner efforts* to attain the victory.

Cathars said: there is no need to read the burial service! Man transiting from the earth must *sing a swan song.* Death is not a punishment but a transition to a higher sphere of divine love which he craved for and has found personally at last!

To reach this degree, an earth-born needs to be prepared by ascending spiritual stairs. Their top is the assumption, the Bridal Bed. The deathbed turns into the *Bridal Bed* and the entrance to the Holy Grail temples is open.

KNIGHTS DID NOT REVEAL SACRED SECRETS UNDER ANY CIRCUMSTANCES

The Inquisition always tried to find out the secret of the Cathar temples. For example, why was a castle built here and not there? They wanted to get keys, tried to find out, drag them off...

There was a strong rumour about the greatest sanctity of the Cathar Grail – the Cypress Casket: a treasure with astronomical maps and topographic schemes of sacred places on the Earth where the greatest secrets could be known.

Glory to the courageous knights who did not give away secrets under any circumstances. A lot of wonders were promised to them and they were also threatened to be killed, but they did not give in! They considered spiritual treasury to be the most beautiful (Alas! we cannot say so about the life of him for whom spirituality is low on his list of priorities).

Catholics tried to imitate Cathars without having a full understanding of the true purpose of celibacy. Why did they need celibacy? Why must the one who is not consecrated to the mystery of the Bridal Bed refrain from sexual relations? In order not be condemned on judgment day? Many Catholics went crazy and some even committed suicide. Then... asylums appeared next to the monasteries on the spots of former Cathar temples.

SWAN LAKE: ENTRANCE INTO THE CHAMBERS OF THE HOLY GRAIL

During Ludwig II's rule medium-sized Swan Lake all of a sudden dried up several times. The water receded and a mysterious entrance was seen (gates to the kingdom of the Holy Grail). But no stranger could enter and even approach it. An invisible force prevented them from entering.

After the death of Ludwig II the lake dried up the following day. The entrance to the chambers of the Grail was opened and Ludwig entered.

The king's body with a heavenly beautiful, royal and noble face rested in a sarcophagus. His soul and spirit went to the Holy Grail while others were discussing how and in what clothes to bury him... Some days later the lake filled up with water again.

INITIATION INTO THE KNIGHTHOOD OF AMOR FINO (FINE LOVE)

The knights of Neuschwanstein called themselves *knighthood of Amor Fino* – exquisite, virginal, lofty, divine love brought to the earth from divine worlds. They dedicated their lives and death to the God of Love to transform the earth.

The knights of the Grail knew that *the mystery of the swan song is in the victory over death.* Love is being refined and multiplied all life long, but there is a level at which it cannot grow. Then there is an *initiation into bigger love* called death... At this supreme moment of separation, a great *swan song* follows which is so enchanting, that defeated death steps back!

The knight of the Holy Grail Ludwig of Bavaria had the courage to battle with Rome face to face. Today he joined in with our lofty Cathar-Templar brotherhood. His wish of transforming the world into a new Neuschwanstein, a swan temple, will at last be fulfilled!

'LET ME SHOW YOU THE TRUE GOLD!'

LUDWIG II OF BAVARIA AND PIOTR TCHAIKOVSKY

In 1876 the young correspondent Tchaikovsky of the newspaper 'Russian Vedomosti' was sent to Bayreuth in Bavaria to the festival in honour of the famous Richard Wagner. The first opera he listened to was 'The Rheingold', which came first in the sequence of 'The Ring of the Nibelung' operas.

The composer was impressed. Sitting in a box he thought about the report that he would write in the evening and send to the newspaper...

There was a knock on the door and King Ludwig himself stood before Tchaikovsky. As the king's box was right opposite the correspondent's box, Ludwig as a spiritually initiated person, *had read* Tchaikovsky and was impressed by his face; he discerned a young Russian genius in the guest.

After a formal exchange of niceties Ludwig asks:

– What do you think about 'The Rheingold'?

– Your majesty, this drama can be expressed deeper.

Ludwig was impressed by his answer; he was peculiarly interested in the fact that plots around the Holy Grail honoured by him could have adequate musical performance expression. The king smiled mysteriously:

– Do you want me to show you *a veritable* the true gold? I invite you to come to my castle tomorrow. On one condition: your arrival will remain a secret. As far as I understand you are a correspondent? Promise me nobody will find out about your visit.

– I promise you, your majesty, – Tchaikovsky answered, bowing to the king.

The next day the composer came to Neuschwanstein. After a short preparation (initiation into the knighthood) he stayed the night in the sacred chambers – and heard a swan song!

One pair of swans succeeds another... Tchaikovsky heard songs one more wonderful than the other and with an abundance of overflowing tears of divine love received *the most supreme initiation into the knighthood of Minne.*

On arrival in Russia no mention was made of his visit to Neuschwanstein and Tchaikovsky wrote the 'Swan Lake' ballet. The scenario of the ballet was absolutely Cathar and one of the knights suggested that Tchaikovsky had been to Ludwig's castle. The *Battle of good against evil and the final triumph of good.* This is the legend of the Holy Grail which is universal both now and always. •

For more detail about the spirituality of Ludwig II of Bavaria and P.Tchaikovsky read 'The Piano as the Lyre of Orpheus' by John Bogomil.

www.cathartemple.org

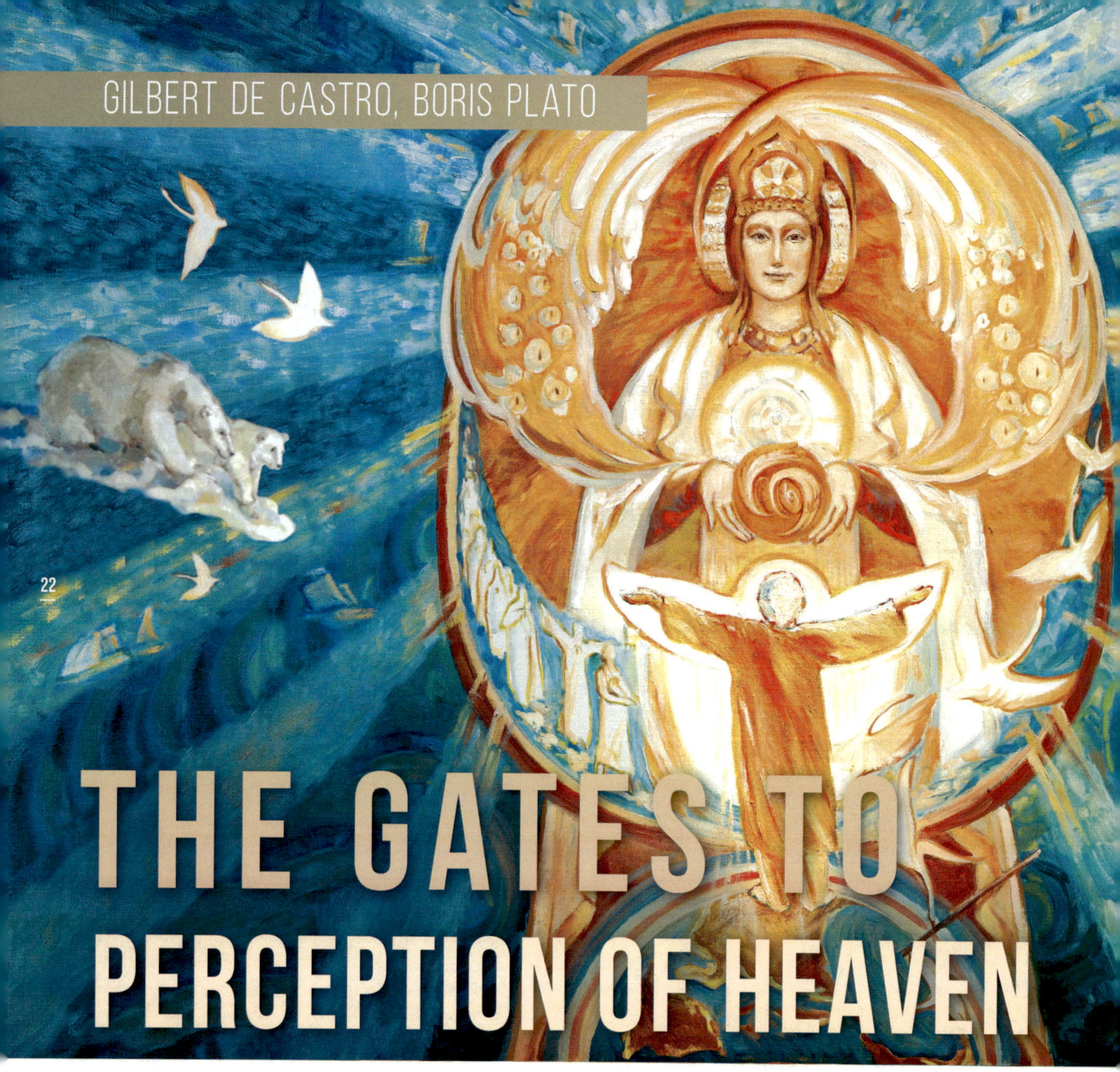

GILBERT DE CASTRO, BORIS PLATO

THE GATES TO PERCEPTION OF HEAVEN

KIND ASTROLOGY OF WHITE NAVIGATORS

Cathars teach about *three main astrological systems.*

The first is *Hyperborean astrology*. It is based on 16 Kind Constellations. Each constellation is an immaculate civilization, which once was on the earth and has left it for mysterious spheres, different dimensions and spaces.

It is not by chance that there are sixteen constellations. On the earth, 15 immaculate civilizations existed in the past and the 16th is preparing to come: the direct connection with the intergalactic Universe!

The supreme deities of kind constellations are the Father and the Mother of pure love, who head the council of kind gods.

The second astrological system (the most common nowadays) consists of 12 tempting constellations which form a *Zodiac* (from the Greek: ‘a circle of

animals'): the horoscope system, which manages the life of homo sapiens. Zodiac network has nothing in common with the divine world. Its spheres are equivocal: good is mixed with evil.

This system is a hologram, built by the Demiurge with a purpose to control and rule over people. It is a cobweb, where humanity has been entrapped.

The secret which even the most consecrated esoterics of the world do not know is that behind the Zodiac resides *the dark astrology of humanoids.* It is concealed and is formed of 22 dark constellations, accursed worlds and dead planets. These are the 22 evil thrones where UFOs come to Earth, revealing forbidden knowledge to mankind: nuclear and biological weapons, artificial diseases, computer and genetic technologies...

The dark astrology is hidden from mankind. Life of the people heads for the Zodiac solely. However, the zodiacal interactions, which commercial astrologists teach about, are nothing but an illusion. Our main task on the earth is to break the dependence on Zodiac, discover the Universe of 16 Kind Constellations and enter the divine world of our true Father and Mother!

ENTRAPPED BETWEEN EARTH AND HEAVEN

What prevents mankind to learn the Universe of our Heavenly Father and Mother is a modern rational science, occult Zodiac astrology and... religion

From the point of view of most religious institutions, even reminding humanity about a kind astrological system is a terrible heresy. In fundamentalist Judaism, Christianity and Islam practicing astrology is considered to be equal to witchcraft. At the same time, for instance, Sufis has a teaching about kind constellations and extraterrestrial worlds. Giordano Bruno, one of the last medieval European Cathars, was burned at the stake for his teaching of cosmic pluralism (or plularity of worlds).

People of religion say: stars do not influence humans whatsoever. God is almighty: both good and evil come from him. He determines the destiny of a soul and sends you either to hell or to paradise. Everything is in his hands, while we are just his slaves...

The mission of the fundamentalist religions of this world is to enslave a man within the material sphere of Earth (in the kingdom of the prince of this world) and after death of physcial body to transfer a soul into the astral trap, of so-called 'afterlife'. Religious devotees are not allowed to study kind worlds. So when a soul leaves the earth, being influenced by the religious teachings, it is captured in the parallel astral world as it does not know where else to go. Biblical paradise and hell are two sides of the same coin: a Sheol.

Till a soul hangs about within the Wheel of Samsara, being entrapped in the astral world in-between the earth and heaven, priceless divine particles are being extracted from it. Influenced by the religious myths and Zodiac programmes, it does not find salvation, but... is being demonized!

THERE ARE HEAVENS, WHICH WAIT FOR US!

It is important to understand that 16 Kind Constellations are not pagan myths or remote cosmic objects from the science fiction films. It is our true Cathar heaven and our destinies where we address our prayers, mediations and contemplation. It is the source, which provides us with spiritual nourishment and reveals the superior heavenly mysteries and secrets to the anointed ones. The Mystical Library of the Universe is situated exactly at the Big Bear constellation.

IT IS NECESSARY TO EXPERIENCE THE ASTROLOGY OF KIND CONSTELLATIONS NOT AS IMAGINARY TEACHING ABOUT OTHER WORLDS, BUT AS AN OPEN ENTRANCE: THE GATES TO PERCEPTION OF HEAVEN. NEW CATHAR EARTH GETS NEW IMMACULATE HEAVENS!

When the heaven of Kind Constellations reveals, the earth breathes with relief. There are heavens, which wait for us, support, send grace, strengthen and open great mysteries to us! We should not ignore them, but discover and enter them spiritually. It means to live according to the unique spheres of each constellation, where beautiful swans, white eagles, lions, immaculate maidens and noble knights are ready to embrace their earthly-born relatives.

Our life is directly and constantly connected with heavenly constellations. We are united. The earth cannot exist without heaven, and vice-versa.

THE TRAGEDY OF THE EARTH CAUSED CATASTROPHES IN MANY OTHER WORLDS

Seven and a half thousand years ago mankind made a catastrophic choice. An enemy of the human race, having called himself a 'lord of the earth' and 'almighty', mesmerized and bent naïve angels of the lower heavens to his will and forced them to pass 180 ethereal operations (of adaptive remodelling) allegedly to reveal the potential of 'other love' (indeed, lust).

THE TRAGEDY OF EARTH, AS REVEALED BY THE QUEEN OF HEAVEN, CAUSED CATASTROPHES IN MANY RELATED WORLDS. THEIR FUTURE DEPENDS ON THE CAPABILITY OF MANKIND TO COPE WITH ATTACKS OF WORLD EVIL.

The consequences of the adaptive remodelling were fatal. The earth under the influence of infernal spheres fell out from the Universe of kind worlds and kind providence. Human beings became a mixture of good and evil, the consciousness was damaged and conscience (the living connection with kind worlds) was lulled. According to the evil plans, it was doomed to become a dead planet, an empty desert after nuclear apocalypse...

Most of the religious doctrines, alas, do not know how to overcome evil. Within their teachings, evil is mixed with good, which is a horrific temptation! Even the slightest mixing of good and evil leads to an utter dominance of evil.

In spite of any distortion, the image of the Heavenly Father and Mother is engraved within the spiritual heart. The connection between mankind and kind worlds remains. It is exceptionally important to keep the authentic image of the Divine Wisdom of kind providence, which expels any evil, in front of your spiritual gaze.

INTRODUCTION TO THE INTERGALACTIC UNIVERSE OF GOOD

During the annual Cathar Congress in October 2013 two unprecedented metahistorical events took place:

(1) 16 Kind Constellations were revealed, and Earth by the merciful will of the Heavenly Queen, was returned into the intergalactic union of good worlds which it once fell out from;

(2) the world axis began to turn towards kindness.

The Queen of Heaven to John Bogomil, 03.10.2013:

'Earth has been accepted into the union of Kind Constellations. Evil, darkness and demonic forces stepped back from it. Who is ready to experience this miracle

According to the ancient Cathar legend, every good soul, when departing from this world, becomes a star. Whereas great spiritual luminaries, when leaving Earth, form entire worlds and good constellations. Such is the mystical connection between the Universe and our planet, which plays a significant role in intergalactic processes!

Three hundred billion stars form just our 'domestic' galaxy of the Milky Way. There are thousands and hundreds of thousands of such galaxies in the Universe... Myriads of solar luminaries look at us kindly and send their admiration and love. Their white ships guard the space above Earth from evil dark forces and share the victorious power of good with mankind.

as the personal revelation, worthy of shedding endless tears of joy?

Introduction of Earth to the Intergalactic Universe of Good will be gradual and will take 5-50 year on the earthly timescale'.

KIND DEITIES SHARE THE CROSS OF MANKIND

The aeon of light will start when Earth enters the Universe of good. This is the reason why UFO chennellers and evil agents block the heaven of 16 Kind Constellations!

Every dark constellation of the Zodiac hides the humanoidal civilization of evil, which attacks Earth, from behind. Fifteen suns from fifteen divine civilizations have already risen above the world. The dawn of the new sun is coming! The solar chariot, shining with the light of Minne, descends and banishes evil from Earth.

The great spiritual battle is being fought. Kind deities share the cross of mankind expelling the evil from the world, advancing commence of the solar aeon. Unlike many channellers, who propose just to wait with indifference until the 'Age of Aquarius' comes, the Divine Wisdom warns mankind: the victory of good and salvation of the world depends on the *victory of each of us over the evil,* mainly – inner evil.

'Thousands of kind constellations are ready to send you invincible knights for help, - says our Heavenly Mother in Her revelations to John Bogomil. – Thousands of worlds look at you with hope as at their possible saviors, similar as mankind looks at white navigators, kind celestial friends of Earth.'

THREE CHALICES IN THE HANDS OF THE QUEEN OF HEAVEN

The Heavenly Queen in her revelations in 1980s-90s spoke about three mystical chalices: *the chalice of sins, chalice of measure and chalice of mercy.*

However, it is not the chalice of sins, which threatens mankind, but the chalice of cumulative evil of dark worlds and civilizations. *Evil is not of the earthly origin!* It is cast upon Earth as a hypnotic dream through the Zodiac. From now on, all evil is being returned to its source!

It is neither Zodiac astrolgical system nor humanoidal forces that govern world processes, but the Kind Providence of our Father. The Apocalyptic Woman clothed with the Sun, Sophia Pronoia[13], is in charge!

When the providentional measure is fulfilled and the time comes, the third chalice will be poured onto the world, the chalice of mercy, light and kindness. It will build the new spiritual society of dominant good in the hearts of people and globally on Earth! •

13 Sofia Pronoia – the Wisdom of 'forethought' (from Greek).

SEEMINGLY ALMOST NOTHING REMAINED OF THE CATHARS AND THERE IS NOT A SINGLE LIVING CATHAR ON EARTH... HOWEVER, I WOULD SAY: THERE IS NOTHING ELSE BUT CATHARISM!

JOHN BOGOMIL

The castle of Peyrepertuse (France) is one of the greatest Cathar relics. Photo by Gleb Nebov, 2015

In 2015 the Association for the Study of the Cathar Culture (Spain) published the book of a modern Spanish researcher, Lohengrin Garcia de Yzaguirre, entitled: 'Cathars of the 21st century on the history of Catharism'. This monograph summarizes the historical knowledge about Cathars and sheds light on the most important aspects of their spirituality, which are put into practice by the modern day Cathar movement. This article is dedicated to some of them.

POLINA ONIPCHUK, LOHENGRIN GARCIA DE YZAGUIRRE

SPAIN

THE CIVILIZATION OF GOOD PEOPLE

CATHARS OF THE 21ST CENTURY ON THE HISTORY OF CATHARISM

Catharism can be boldly called a unique precedent of a divine civilization that took place across Europe. Alas! Almost nothing is known about the solar civilization of good people and what is known has almost completely been taken from denunciations of the Inquisition. The spiritual movement which covered all Europe in the 9-13th centuries was erased and sealed.

In the 1980s, the Vatican archives were partially opened and an entire good universe from the Cathar civilization was revealed in front of the stunned researchers. Since those times, a spiritual movement, which can be called a Cathar Renaissance, has started spreading all over Europe. This is the first sign of a new epoch. 700 years later, the martyrs have returned to defeat their oppressors. The laurel has blossomed – the Cathars are descending to the world!

FAITH IN THE GOOD DIVINITY

In medieval Catholic sources there is often mentioned that Cathars believed in 'two gods - one good and the second wicked...', but in accordance with the opinion of the majority of academic authors, in particular of Jean Duvernoy, such a view is simplified and preconceived.

Cathar dualism presupposed *absolute immixability of good and evil*[14]. 'God is love', they said, 'and His kingdom is out of this world'. Having created this world 'that lies in evil', Satan proclaimed himself as its god known as Elohim, the God of the Old Testament.

From a Cathar point of view, all souls regardless of profession, nationality, and gender are equal and have divine origin. Cathars believed neither in mortal torments nor in the Last Judgment and thought all souls serve their time in an earthly hell during many lives, until they awaken and return to their heavenly fatherland.

14 See Matt, 7:18: A good tree cannot bring forth evil fruit, neither can a corrupt tree bring forth good fruit.

CATHARISM IN THE MIDDLE AGES

Historians believe Catharism emerged in the 9th century and spread in a short time across entire Europe from the Rhine to the Pyrenees and further on: to Occitania (the South of modern France), Lombardy, Italy, the German principalities, Catalonia, the north of France, Flanders, Hungary, Bohemia, the Mediterranean coast from Italy to Spain, England, and the Balkans (Bogomils).

At least 20 Cathar churches and orders are known. Catharism became wide-spread in Occitania, Lombardy, Tuscany and Champagne. In the first two regions Catharism existed (with a rare exception) at least until the second decade of the 14th century.

From the very beginning Catharism and Bogomilism were persecuted by the Byzantine hierarchy in the east and by the Roman in the west. The only exceptions were Bosnia which adopted Bogomilism as its state religion in 1199, and neighbouring Serbia and Dalmatia. They remained Bogomil until mid-15th century.

Between 1167 and 1176 at the initiative of the Toulouse community and Carcassonne community, in the castle of Saint Felix de Karaman (now Saint-Felix-Lorage) – a Cathar council took place, in which the representatives of 16 communities (churches) of France, Spain, Greece, Bulgaria, Dalmatia, and Asia Minor participated. At the council various spiritual questions were resolved, and the structure of the Cathar Church in Occitania was organized and Bogomil patriarch of Constantinople, Nicetas I, ordained the first Cathar Perfects.

Aristocrats, priests, monks, ordinary citizens, merchants, craftsmen, cultivators, elegant ladies, and female peasants followed the Cathars... Whole cloisters were converted into Catharism! Some Catholic bishops received consolamentum on their deathbed.

Later, in times of persecution, many Catholics refused to deliver 'heretics' to the Inquisition, saying they were good neighbours and their good brothers.

BY THE END OF THE 12TH CENTURY CATHARISM WAS PROFESSED BY PERHAPS ONE THIRD OF THE EUROPEAN POPULATION. BY SOME EVALUATIONS, CATHAR BELIEVERS NUMBERED FROM 200,000 TO 1,000,000 IN OCCITANIA ALONE.

THE PURE AND PERFECT ONES

The word 'cathar' (*katharos*, 'pure' in Greek) was coined by the Roman inquisitors. Cathars themselves preferred to be called Good Men (*Bons Homes*) or good Christians.

In the Cathar brotherhood several steps of consecration were distinguished: the stage of newcomer in the faith (novices), sympathizers or listeners (*acusticoi*). Mercy, forgiveness, obedience, truthfulness, fast, abstinence and faithfulness were practiced at the stage of believers (*credenti*).

To become an 'advanced' credent, one had to pass ordeals. The one who passed them could pronounce the 'Lord's Prayer' and wear spiritual garments (black or blue, rarely green coloured). The believers were still considered as being in captivity of evil and therefore required spiritual guidance of the Perfect. These pupils of Cathar Perfects were called John or Joanna.

The Perfect (*Perfeit*) or Good Men (*Bons Homes and Bones Donas*)[15] received Holy Spirit at the sacrament of consolamentum. The one wishing to become Perfect took the vow of obedience to Perfects in a Cathar community during one or two years. During consolamentum the ordained took the vow never to lie, swear, kill any living being, taste animal food (with the exception of fish), give in to carnal passions (to live in perfect purity and virginity), and not to travel alone, as well as a vow of readiness to undergo persecution and death for the sake of love of the Heavenly Father.

Afterwards a companion – a sworn brother (*soci* according to the Occitan way) – from whom he did not separate while travelling and ministry, was assigned to the new Perfect.

The practice of *consolamentum* was also widely disseminated – the mysteries of consolation of the dying ones as preparation and soul cleansing before a transfer to eternity.

Those who were freed from the remodeling of the prince of this world were called Pure. Those who entered the workshop of modeling by Holy Spirit were called Perfect. The stages of the Anointed and Immortal followed, and were carefully hidden from the Inquisition.

CHURCH OF LOVE

The Cathar movement comprised estate churches, like the early Christian ones. Cathar houses (*bastides*) – spiritual communities of Good Men and Good Women headed by elders of both sexes – were their foundation.

15
In the Occitan language

> IF YOU ASK THEM, NOBODY COULD BE MORE CHRISTIAN. AS FOR THEIR SPEECHES, NOBODY WOULD DESERVE TO BE LESS BLAMED, AND WHAT THEY TALK ABOUT IS CONFIRMED BY DOINGS. AS FOR THE MORALITY OF THESE HERETICS, THEY DO NOT DECEIVE ANYONE, OPPRESS ANYONE, NOR BEAT ANYONE.
>
> *Bernard of Clairvaux*

When the Cathar community grew in a sufficient degree and was ready, it reorganized into a church: A bishop and deacons were elected among the Perfect. Cathar bishops, in constant care for their congregation, travelled, helping the faithful to ascend in purity and perfection.

Cathar communities were open to society. They accepted both Perfects travelling from other towns and believers who wished to immerse into Cathar doctrines. Communities lived on donations, from various professions and from the upbringing of children. They dedicated themselves to ministry for patients. There were up to 70 or more Cathar communities in some cities.

AMOR VS. ROMA[16]

Cathars denied the effectiveness of the Catholic sacraments, especially if the priest administering them was found sinning. They refused to baptize little children, they believed the person should make a conscious choice. They also denied the Catholic sacrament of confession, the sacrament of marriage which just then was introduced by papacy, and Eucharist. They turned against the crucifix cult and did not recognize the Catholic Blessed Virgin Mary.

THE CATHARS REVEALED ANOTHER DEITY - THE KINDEST FATHER GOD AND THE HEAVENLY MOTHER BEARING IN PURITY AND IMPECCABILITY; ANOTHER CHRIST AND ANOTHER CHURCH, ANOTHER HOLY GRAIL, ANOTHER CONFESSION – DEEP CATHARSIS WITH COMPLETE AND EFFECTIVE PURIFICATION OF THE INNER BEING, ANOTHER MARRIAGE: THEOGAMY, ANOTHER CROSS – A SOLAR INSTRUMENT OF DEIFICATION, AND THE KNIGHTS' SWORD FOR VICTORY OVER EVIL.

Cathars did not need altars – the heavenly Bridegroom himself came to the Cathar agapes and performed the liturgy of the Grail around a Round Table, nourishing the ordained with myrrhic compounds. At these intakes of love the Cathar perfect blessed bread, covering it with white cloth and dividing it into pieces for all the attendees; after which communicants gave each other 'a kiss of peace'. We believe this tradition goes back to the most ancient colliriada of Nightingale Mountain – the communion of Mother of God with sacred flatbread with the face of the Mother of God engraved on them[17].

CATHARISM AND SOCIETY

It is difficult to overestimate the influence of Catharism on the development of Occitan society. Dwellers of Occitania in the 11-13th centuries had freedoms and privileges unheard of for that epoch. Many historians are of the opinion that it was Catharism which laid the foundations of the modern European democracy!

Occitania got political, judicial and municipal liberty; freedom of word and of trade (without a predominance of taxes and duties); and freedom of conscience, which was especially precious. Politics and religion were separated.

The cultural flowering of that time is connected in the first place with troubadours, originators of European poetry. The singers of *Amor Fino*, Fine Love, were mostly

16
'Amor versus Roma' (Latin.) – Love versus Rome.
In Russia they said Mir (Peace) versus Rim (Rome).

17
About the Cathar sacrament of the Colliriada read the article of John Bogomil "Colliriada: the bread of deities" ("Catharism XXI". Issue No.1" 2015, p. 18).

converted to Catharism. One can say the Cathars found in poetry and music the loftiest and most spiritual way of the spreading of universal statutes of peace, kindness and love.

THE ALBIGENSIAN CRUSADE

In the 11-12th centuries, the persecution of Cathars by the Catholic Church was not wide-spread. The battle was conducted mainly in the form of theological disputes which the Romans lost most often. At that time Catharism gained ever greater recognition among people and Rome, being seriously worried, decided to resort to an argument of strength.

The crusade against the Cathars which Pope Innocent III called in 1209 received the name of 'Albigensian' (with reference to the town of Albi). The barons of France and Europe who responded to the appeal attacked Toulouse's county lands and the viscounty of Trencavel. The crusade was led by the papal legate Arnaud Amaury, prior of Citeaux, and later by Simon de Montfort.

Savage repressions against civil population became the characteristic of this campaign (Bezier in 1209, Marmande in 1219), as well as the massive mass burnings of heretics – Minerva (140 persons burnt in 1210), Lavaur (400 burnt in 1211). But the local population, for which the war bore national liberation as well as a religious character, actively resisted the crusaders and supported local nobility.

In 1220 it became finally clear that the attempt to implant the Catholic dynasty of the Monforts in Toulouse and Carcassonne failed.

The situation changed after King of France Louis VIII intervened in the war in 1226, followed after his death by Louis IX. The region was reconquered by 1229 and local nobility agreed to a temporary armistice.

The Cathar communities took refuge clandestinely, but they remained very numerous.

Military actions ceased only in 1255. In the course of the Albigensian wars around one million died (counting victims from both sides).

THE INQUISITION

The Inquisition was created by a council in 1215 and it was dependent on bishops. It was refounded by the papacy in 1231 as a constantly functioning religious tribunal independent from local bishops. The investigations were based on the systematic denunciations, as well as on the confessions that were used as testimonies. This system managed to destroy Catharism during the lifetime of several generations.

The punishments introduced by inquisitors differentiated from the wearing of yellow crosses sewn on clothes to a confiscation of property and life imprisonment. The death sentence was executed by means of transferring a convict to the hands of temporal power, and was applied to perfects who refused to renounce their 'delusions', as well as for believers who 'relapsed into heresy'. Those who died in 'heretical abomination' were sentenced to exhumation and incineration of remains, and their houses – to destruction.

> “THERE ARE TWO CHURCHES. ONE CHURCH IS PERSECUTED AND FORGIVES. THE OTHER CHURCH PURSUES AND BURNS AT THE STAKE”
>
> *Peire Autier, a Cathar Perfect in the early 14th century*

MONTSÉGUR

After the signing of the Paris agreement, in accordance with which the count of Toulouse obeyed the king of France, the hierarchs of the Cathar churches of Toulouse, the Agenois and Razes addressed the owner of a little reinforced village on mountain Montségur. A request was made to Raymond de Perella to allow them to build there ‘the altar and the heart (focus) of the Church’. He agreed and from 1232 to 1243 missions from the Cathar Houses of Montségur were sent for clandestine sermons and the ministry of sacraments.

In 1243 Montségur was besieged by the army of the king of France. What happened next is cloaked in secrecy. According to the Roman sources, the siege lasted for almost a year. On March 16, 1244, two hundred Perfects, as well as twenty from the garrison of the castle, who had joined voluntarily, were burned at the foot of the mountain...

The Montsegur Perfects revealed themselves in 2007 to John Bogomil and testified: ‘None of us burned in the fire. *Our executioners burned!*’

Oh! What majestic sight was the blissful and beautiful descent of two hundred Perfect ones in white clothes headed by Christ with the Chalice in his hands...

The crusaders lost their speech, they froze paralyzed. The Lamb of crucified love, the crowned King of the Anointed ones, led His faithful ones, as a flock of white swans, to the Bridal Supper. And the prepared souls went without fearing anything, in a most high ecstasy. They ascended the stake with the words ‘God is love!’ and on a fiery chariot flew to the palaces of the divine Bridegroom.

And the fire of the stake was thrown on inquisitors standing nearby! Panic, horror, shrill wails began. Only one managed to survive, but he became half-witted afterwards. This is the story of the place at the base of Montsegur, still called ‘Camp dels cremats’, the Field of the burned.

The Cathar castle of Montségur, France.
View of the Field of burned.
Cathar Fire Wedding was held here in 1244.
Photo: Makariy Parfenov, 2007.

THE LAST CATHARS

By the end of the 13th century Catharism had almost ceased to exist in Occitania. But Peire Autier, a former notary from Aix les – Termes, close to Count Roger-Bernard de Foy, in 1299 headed a small group of Good Men 'steadfast in their determination for the preaching of the Cathars to be renewed in its former territories'. Among them was his brother Guillaume Autier and his son Jaume. With the remains of Cathar clandestinity, they managed to 'kindle the fire of Catharism from Quercy to the Pyrenees for a little while'.

The attempt of the 'reconquest of the brothers Authieux' continued from 1300 to 1310 thanks to the increased number of catacomb pastors. But the Inquisition caught and burned one after another all underground preachers. Jaume and Guillaume Autier were burned in Carcassonne in 1309. Amiel de Perle and Peire Autier were burned in Toulouse in 1310.

The only ones who managed to escape into Catalonia were Guillaume Belibaste and Philippe d'Alayrc. After Philippe's death, Belibaste was betrayed by a double agent, seized and burned in 1321 by the order of the archbishop of Narbonne. The prophecy he uttered during the execution came to us: *'In 700 years from now the laurel will become green again.'*

THE LAUREL TURNS GREEN!

One can KILL THE PEOPLE, BUT ONE CAN NOT DESTROY LOVE. One may not muzzle the mouth of the eternal Word, it is impossible to forbid the breath and action of the Spirit of God. The Cathar church did not vanish, but, like the Grail, left to afterlife in expectation of its hour.

Modern mankind is found in deep crisis which covers all aspects of its existence.
In these complex times the Cathars return to Earth, stretching out a helping hand and offering golden keys to the archetypal morality of kindness, purity, and love for the salvation of the world. And it depends on us to accept them and implement the solar design of a divine civilization on Earth, the reality of which is confirmed by the life and testimony of thousands of Cathar martyrs of love. •

PETRO DOROGA

A WRITER, A MEMBER OF
THE INTERNATIONAL PEN-CLUB (UKRAINE)

THE RUSSIAN SCENERY AFTER THE BATTLE

Review on the book
'Alma Mater Dei et Humani and invalidushki (disabled veterans) on Valaam.'
by John Bogomil.

All books of John Bogomil are surprisingly musical and they sound incessantly. At times quiet, or lofty; sometimes tragic, but more often optimistic...

When you take any of his books in your hands, you experience it as a musical instrument.

A violin-book, an organ-book, an oboe-book, a flute-book, a piano-book...

However, in this book there is a voice of silence, and an abyss shrouds this silence.

It is the abyss of inscrutable depth, of grief, of Solovki. Eternal one.

While you leaf through the pages, you go deep into silent infinity. It seems that the fingers and hands of lots of cripples and disabled veterans hold this large-tonnage in silence.

They hold it as the Atlases hold Earth.

Without groans, sighs, complaints, murmur, or curses.

You can only hear a tear running down the cheek of the planet.

It is the tear of the Divine Mother.

Valaam island. View from the Ladoga shore ►

THE GULAG WITHIN THE GULAG

A little book, actually a brochure, *'Alma Mater Dei et Humani and invalidushki (disabled veterans) on Valaam'* has accumulated megatons of pain in itself and has grown to galactic proportions.

What is this Earth, where we are doomed to live?

It is a concentration camp.
So what if in this concentration camp, a person is sent to the Gulags?

A horror multiplied by despair.

The Gulag... within the Gulag?

It is beyond comprehension. The mind refuses to interpret, or analyze. Even the soul falls silent, flowing into tears...

This book is written with tears, like a crystal chalice filled up with eyewater.

'STUMPS'

The impulse for these writings, was inspired by portraits of the artist Gennady Dobrov, who visited Valaam in mid-1970s and created the series of unique images of disabled veterans of the Second World War.

How did they get there, 'in the depth of Siberian mines'?

By Stalin's order they were moved there by force, so that they *'would not mar a landscape and hinder the propaganda's death machine'* which praised war as a beautiful heroism.

They carried disabled veterans away ... in the best case. The majority were shot, exterminated, tormented and wiped off the face of the earth.

> *'The true picture was this. Time was getting short: it was the tyrant's birthday. An order came to gather 75 thousand innocent martyrs of the Second World War and shoot them all - literally in a few hours(!!!)*
>
> *There were not enough rifle-men of the paramilitary guard! Try to get rid of dozens of thousands of innocent people just in three hours! An immediate mobilization was required to organize new shooting squads.*
>
> *Former brother-soldiers of victims were ordered to shoot the disabled veterans... Do you see? They had to shoot their own combat comrads, whom they had shared their bread and cross with, gave their lives for, and faced death together, defending the Fatherland... Their heroes, instead of being honoured as Olympic gods, they,'stumps' (some of them were without arms, or legs, others blind or semi-deaf), were born (not even led, born) to be shot!*
>
> *Some of them were lugged to the shooting on the stretcher. They were kissing each other and weeping bitter tears.*
>
> *That is how the Fatherland treated its saviours!*
>
> *Mankind had not yet known such a massacre. It was the Gulag within the Gulag...'*

I recall from the memory of my father how he was secretly telling my mother about the horrible mopping-up of which he became an accidental witness, when poor 'stumps' and 'samovars' were thrown into patrol wagons and taken away in an unknown direction. My father knew, it was to their certain death, as in 1930s the same happened to kobza and bandura players in Ukraine. His elder brother too lost his leg in that infernal world war and disappeared somewhere abroad...

A SERMON FROM THE HEART OF THE FOLK SOUL

How many of them, the disabled veterans of the Second World War were there?

> *'According to the official statistics only, there were two million six hundred thousand of permanently disabled. Taking into consideration concentration camps in Spain, Germany and USSR, there were more than seven million prisoners! After 1945, almost every third was a defenseless cripple with amputated extremities, hearing aids, shell-shocked or blind.'*
>
> *'The terrible campaign to exile the war heroes, armless and legless, with their wooden pieces for the disabled, lasted until the tyrant's death. The statistics are inexorable. In 1951, up to 100,000 veterans were banished. In 1952, another battle against heroes took place. In 1953 (year of Stalin's death) even more were exiled... In total, 180 thousand of sacrificial lambs of Russia were sent to concentration camps for certain death!!!*
>
> *They were not dying, no. They were immortal! Good wins over evil. They have not gone anywhere and are still alive today. However, instead of poor hands they have little wings, and, instead of poor legs, they have their own thrones near the Good God.'*

It is difficult to define the genre of this book.

A Solovki sermon from the heart of the folk soul?

A legend about warriors of light?

A bird's liturgy?

A tragic epos?

It is all correct... However, even together, they do not reflect the pain enclosed in the text. This pain is more burning, more everlasting, beyond the grasp of mind, impossible to determine with human language.

Documentary drawings of Gennady Dobrov ▶ (1937-2011) are used in "Alma Mater Dei et Humani and invalidushki on Valaam".

The cry, the tear, the despair in the night, the pain, the torment, the lacerated wound, the torn off hands, or the lost legs, lost eyes... – beyond the verge of the expressible.

It is possible to write about that. There are enough words in the language to express it, but there are such states of mind before which words genuflect.

THEY NOT ONLY SURVIVED – THEY TRANSFORMED INTO LIVING RELICS!

> “ *'They had been keeping the disabled for ten years on Valaam as criminals and then abandoned them. They treated them in the following way: the quicker they would die the better. They made them drunk with industrial alcohol, fed them with rotten meat and spoiled pap rich in worms.*
>
> *'The stumps' without hands and feet were placed in special barracks. They were beaten up. They were placed into big baskets and hung on trees – 'to breathe in air'. They suffered unsustainably, hanging for several days riddled with bedsores, then forgotten about.*
>
> *And they survived for decades! Oh, miracle – in such horrible conditions. They did not only survive – they were transformed into living relics! How is that possible?! The torturers drank hard; and the cripples became lively relics and were fragrant.'*

The language of this book (I consider it to be a book, and not a brochure, but a huge volume!) is tender, soft, merciful with a lot of endearment suffixes: handies, leggies, mummy, invalidushki, pinkies, toothie. It is the only way to transmit, at least in part, a cordial sob, a tear that stuck in the throat...

MANKIND PASSED THEM BY

It sounds frightening and even wild, but all 'great' writers of the 20th century, the 'powerful and glorious' Russian literature ignored these disabled persons' tragedies. Well, you say literature?! All Russia passed by it. Mankind passed by them. *'Nobody knows them today: authorities erased them from memory. The disabled are a disgrace for villains.'*

And Russian intellectuals passed with blind eyes by the reproductions of Gennady Dobrov *(what a wonderful surname – means 'kind')*. Only the Kirghiz world-famous classical writer Chingiz Aitmatov wrote: *'I literally fell ill. All night long I did not sleep. I would send out these copies worldwide.'*

But he did not send them, although he had millions of readers and fans.

This labour was taken over by John Bogomil himself.

A prophet perfect in word.

With a martyr's soul and Solovki-like vision.

With the hearing of Solovki.

And with the heart born again in Solovki.

And with the word burned by fierce frosts of Solovki.

VICTORS IN THE THIRD WORLD WAR BETWEEN GOOD AND EVIL

> *'I will describe how many of them became disabled persons.*
>
> *Appointed to penal battalions, they were sent against German tanks with almost bare hands: just with a bottle of 'Molotov cocktail' (a fire bomb). Do you remember the heroic deed near Dubosekovo, Moscow region, during the WWII? Soldiers fought against German tanks without weapon at all! The German tankmen were deranged: they could not shoot unarmed... That is why the Germans were discouraged and fled from the battlefield: their opponents did not fear armed soldiers, tanks, or planes; many did not fear even death. The great courage of martyrs of the Second Golgotha - future 'stumps' and 'samovars' – overwhelmed and paralysed Germans.*
>
> *They won the Second World War. Honour and glory to them! They will win the third one as well, which will not be an earthly war, but the supramundane clash of good and evil.'*

This book teaches to scorn death.

It teaches how to overcome death not only by dying, but also by the sacrifice of martyrdom, extended for half a century and more.

The spiritual phenomenon of Solovki is incomprehensible without understanding the tragic essence of a human life. This subject is central in literature and philosophy. A lot of books are dedicated to it… and yet nobody understood it so profoundly as John Bogomil.

Great sufferings give rise to great questions.

A book 'Alma Mater Dei et Humani and disabled persons on Valaam' by John Bogomil.

Who are they, these martyrs, cripples without kith or kin, persecuted and hungry, holy fools, forgotten by everyone?

Are they the people's Christs?

Are they bird-like minstrels?

Are they sacrificed lambs of the Second Golgotha?

Are they Hyperborean deities?

Yes they are. However, the words fade again facing the abyss of a universal suffering and grief.

THE HIGHER THE HEAVENLY DESTINY OF A SOUL, THE MORE EXCRUCIATING IS ITS EARTHLY LIFE

The sufferings must tell us that soul is immortal.

Therefore, the earth is just a place of its making.

The more delicate and pure the soul is, the higher is its celestial destiny and the more excruciating the earthly path it passes.

John Bogomil managed to see the grace present in suffering.

How is that possible? – a surprised reader will cry out – is that conceivable?

For instance, let's quote Russian writer Maksim Gorky:

'I am the old hater of both physical and moral suffering. Both, considered subjectively and objectively, arouse indignation, disgust, and even anger within me. Suffering must be hated, only this way you can destroy it. It is humiliating Man, a great and tragic creature...'
(from the letter to K. Fedin)

John Bogomil has a radically different view, deeper and more touching:

> *'The significance of suffering of a person, apart from personal transfiguration and revelation of the heavenly love, is the great expiation of the earth.*
>
> *The penal battalion soldiers, prisoners, the disabled made their feats in order that evil, vice, cruelty, injustice, misanthropy, wars, contempt for people, magic and witchery abandon the world... The most defenseless and persecuted became the saviours of the entire planet from the pest of fascism. The heroes defeated the outrageous evil of dark worlds!'*

'LIFE IS ONGOING THANKS TO THE HEROIC DEEDS OF UNKNOWN MARTYRS...'

The cross is the sign of the earth.

Let us hearken, and discover the great secret and the holy truth

> *'Why do souls come to Earth? To find happiness, have family, children? No! They descend to be consecrated to the mystery of the Cross. Receive your sight, blind ones! Man comes to carry his cross with dignity and obtain ineffable beatitudes. This is the Cathar, or the Divine Mother's vision.'*

You will not need a pencil to write down countless aphorisms and profound truths while reading this book. Divine Wisdom is being engraved on the heart by itself and remains in memory forever.

> *'There are no victors in the wars, but there are innocent victims, and there are millions of them.'*
> *'Any spiritual battle is always a battle of good and evil, a clash of two mentalities: philanthropic (kind) and misanthropic (evil).'*
> *'Try to go into a battle with the fear of death, and you will be the first to receive a bayonet stab in the heart.'*
>
> *'Nothing is needed for happiness, but Minne.'*
>
> *'Nobody can do evil to you, if you do not wish it to happen."*
>
> *'Learn to see Christ in your near ones.'*
>
> *'Life is ongoing thanks to the heroic deeds of unknown martyrs.'*

I am a weak man. Hesitation is my eternal companion. How often I experience great internal struggle, following John Bogomil and conceiving his Cathar teaching! It is not easy for me at times to accept some of his thoroughgoing statements...

How can I speak about myself, when even Father John is not guaranteed to be free from doubt and pain!

Only religious fanatics do not know hesitations or heart discord.

While the great devotees experience this:

> *'The heaviest crisis after writing a book...'*
>
> *'I went through a difficult time, believe me...'*

However '*Alma Mater Dei et Humani and invalidushki on Valaam*' gives the reader a confidence that the prophet is right, it increases trust in what he says, urges to support and follow him.

This book is not only a repentant prayer tribute to great martyrs. Each phrase and every single word of this book examine the world in mercy, compassion, kindness and humanism.

Its mission is high and great.

A Divine mission. •

JONATHAN WHITE

THE TUTORESS OF HOLINESS

The cloud of the Divine Mother's grace from Athos rested on the eldress Euphrosinia of Pochaiv (1916-1993). The breath of the true Bogomil faith emanated from her. Everything she did was sweet and blissful: be it a dialogue or a prayer, prostrations or ablution at a holy well... Even her weaknesses and spiritual battles were covered by ineffable bliss. She was filled with awe, and was always craving for Christ.

The monks of the Lavra hated, persecuted and offended her. Sometimes they beat her... She never complained or condemned her offenders. She cried gently, scrutinizing the scars of beating, and thanked God with tears. She believed the sufferings she endured were a gift and honour.

She craved for ascending new stages of acquisition of the All-Holy Spirit. She said about herself: 'I have acquired the second stage and now I am approaching the third one'... And how many are they in all? About fifteen hundred?

After many 40-day bread-and-water fasts, which she kept in her earthly days, including heroic deeds of reciting psalms continually, innumerable sacrifices for love, night vigil prayers, and battles with the prince of this world, Euphrosinia achieved the spiritual level of *a great anointed* one and entered the pantheon of the immortals after her fiery crises.

... In her earthly days she remembered that when she was three years old, she heard that all people die and exclaimed with all her heart: 'I will never die!' She craved to enter the gates of immortality which she received through Catharism.

Several years after her decease, those who opened her coffin, gasped with surprise, for her imperishable relics were literally coated with myrrh!

ENCYCLOPEDIA OF CATHARISM

Since 1998 Mother Euphrosinia has been giving revelations at her relics in a Bogomil community. Her posthumous spiritual instructions have formed an encyclopedia of unique Cathar knowledge. Euphrosinia lights up the candle of heavenly love Minne in hearts and opens the gates of true spirituality, which consists, primary, of knowing the Divine Mother through direct personal experience.

We used to know Mother Euphrosinia as a hermitess, a catacomb woman of prayer, who entered the fiery sphere of the All-Good All-Holy Spirit; a weeper, who bemoaned with hot tears those who were not able to enter into the light of love of the Father... Today we are called to meet new Euphrosinia: a deity, clothed with the sun of beatitudes of Minne.

Euphrosinia is a goddess of New Atlantis, the Queen of solarization of a person. She is the spiritual Mother of a new divine humanity, who lights up the ever-burning candle of Minne.

In order to defeat the Evil One, like mother Euphrosinia, you need fire. A spiritual hero goes through white fonts of purification, overcomes lustful temptations of the prince of this world and kindles in the heart a lamp which gradually turns into an ever-burning candle. With each passing day the fire of this mysterious candle must be ignited brighter and brighter.

Ignite within us the ever-burning lamp of pure love, eldress Euphrosinia! As you are Clothed with the Sun, clothe us in the Sun of beatitudes of Minne. Lead us into the mysterious spheres of divine existence and teach us to be nourished by the golden cross of kindness and from the tree of the original immaculacy.

Give us new birth in immortal bodies with immaculate compositions, and imperishable garments! •

WHAT HAS HAPPENED IN THE HIGHEST

THE HEAVENLY EXHORTATIONS OF MOTHER EUPHROSINIA (1998-2011)

What grace is here! If I had lived till today, I would never have descended from Montsegur. Here, there are relics of thousands of martyrs. Here is the Chalice of our sweetest Christ. Here, there are thousands of springs, like the holy spring in Pochaiv[18]. What grace was at the font on Pochaiv Hill, so the same is here, all across Montsegur, and even greater.

All saints of the world gather here, in pakibytie[19]. That is why those who visit this sacred place are bestowed with the blessing of all saints of the true spirit - the spirit of the Holy Grail.

Those whom I call 'of the true spirit' belong to the Church of the Holy Grail. The Chalice of the Most High was revealed to you thanks to my blessing. At first, it was revealed to me in Heaven and then – to you.

Perceive the revelation of the Holy Grail to you as the continuation of my relics. In the beginning, my relics were revealed as a sign of the Cathar grace, and then the Holy Grail and the Cathars revealed themselves.

ABOUT THE SECOND CONVERSION

My child, the expression 'second conversion'[20] was not invented by you.

I was astounded when the Immortals of San Salvador showed me the Cathar treasure of mysteries. My old faith and Amphilokhiy's[21] school of the acquisition of the Holy Spirit turned out to be a kind of childish prattle, because the truth and genuine mysteries of the Cathar Church, opened to me, were so great!

Cathar fathers and mothers took me under their patronage.

Somewhat more than three months (according to earthly chronology) I was in obedience to one of the greatest myrrhophoras (holy women) of the Cathar Church, Mother-Superior Matillana.

I remember the anointed ones of San Salvador answered my question: how to achieve their spiritual level in a short space of time?

– Through the second conversion.

My child, I accepted the second conversion. As in former times I had resolutely rejected the sovietdom, stalinism, communist ideology and atheism, so then I rejected Byzantine Christianity as the most dreadful delusion ever.

Just imagine, what effort it required from me, how lonely I felt! Believe me, a million times more lonely than during my earthly life.

When you accepted the second conversion in the 'desert of Peyrepertuse'[22], I stood behind you and I strengthened you.

How happy I was to accept the second conversion! I

18
Pochaiv is a town in Ukraine, where John Bogomil met Mother Euphrosinia for the first time.

19
Pakibytie (or palingenesis) is the blissful otherworldly sphere between earth and heaven.

20
The second conversion means to reject the corrupted images of faith (religious) and return to the genuine and universal spirituality.

21
Amphilokhiy of Pochaiv was the spiritual guide of Mother Euphrosinia in her earthly days.

22
The **'Desert of Peyrepertuse'** is the name for a dramatic episode on the spiritual path of John Bogomil, which happened near the Cathar castle of Peyrepertuse (France) when he accepted the second conversion.

HEAVENS, IS ONLY ABOUT TO COME TO EARTH

lost nothing. Love and proximity of the Mother of God, gifts of the Holy Spirit, asceticism, bowing, fasting – the Perfect fathers had it all and even more.

I had been in absolute obedience to them like a small child for a long time, until I acquired their spirit and advanced quickly.

Today I am delighted to belong to the rank of Pure and Perfect myrrhophoras in the retinue of the Most Holy Virgin, who is the eternal Patroness of the Church of pure people.

THE HOLY SPIRIT IN ATLANTIS

The Holy Spirit embodied in Atlantis as a beautiful young King (how it was revealed to John Bogomil at Olympus). Holy Spirit the Divinizer, who was understood in Atlantis as the sum of divine energies of the higher cosmos, personified in Atlanteans when the Father became apparent in Christ and Christ became apparent in his dedicated followers.

The teaching about the acquisition of the Holy Spirit comes not from Jerusalem, but is of Atlantean origin. Therefore there is not a single word in elohimic scriptures, either in the Torah or gospels.

Whereas Mother Euphrosinia, as well as other glorious acquisitors of the Holy Spirit, taught only about the mystery of the acquisition of the Holy Spirit, being directly inspired and guided from on high, from Atlantis.

O the sweetest Chalice of Atlantis!

How to acquire the Holy Spirit in an Atlantean way? – you may ask.

The Holy Spirit is acquired as you dissociate with the patterns of the adaptive remodeling (corruption). Only then it becomes possible for us (your heavenly patrons) to purify the composition of Adamites from the poisonous part.

ABOUT THE SPIRITUAL PATH

The Queen of Heaven asked me to tell you that sins are forgiven quickly in the end times, but a *feat of prayer is required*, because prayer is extremely laborious, and it is almost impossible to break through devilish dark clouds.

A sin which formerly could be forgiven after five or ten years of obedient life, now can be atoned just with a few weeks of prayer.

Do not breathe a word of love, those, who do not want to see yourselves soberly.

The Church has disavowed virginity. That is why there are so many troubles. Return to virginity and live a holy life. The Most Holy Virgin, Her personal image and example will serve you as guarantee of rescue.

I used to say in my earthly days: some people have been visiting church for fifty years and prayed, however the Lord will ask them:

'What have you been doing in the temple, if you did not atone for any of your sins by prayer?'

It is a great mystery to be introduced to the heavenly temple while being on the earth, for which an elder-guide full of grace is required. Peace and bliss to you, whose spiritual father and mother are able to open the gates of the Kingdom.

Do not limit your interest to my teachings and to abstract curiosity, but do according to my words.

It is incorrect to think that the holy path, which I have proposed, is for a few. This path is intended for all mankind. However, it should be open to people to a variable extent. Some will follow it entirely and will gain the crowns, while the others – let them follow as they can, however, for them not to fall into deception, all steps and acts should be blessed from above. No prostration should be done without the blessing of the spiritual father!

THE VOW OF SPIRITUAL VIRGINITY

The vow of spiritual virginity is essential on the earth, because it is impossible to love purely and divinely, unless you are a virgin. Otherwise love becomes impure, and uncountable temptations will occur.

I thank you, my dear children, on behalf of the Blessed Virgin for taking the vows of eternal joy (how the vows of virginity are called in heaven). Be more and more zealous of acquisition of the Divine Spirit, Adorer and Divinizer!

It is not books, that convert people, but a prayer of intercession for them, sober repentance and fiery zeal of the messengers. Do not lose discernment and the gift of spiritual introspection. Carefully read the mysteries of the inner man and fearlessly free yourself from transitory chimeras.

*

Teach about virginity all over the world as (1) the key for salvation in the end times, (2) entry into the ineffable Bridal Chamber, which was promised by our Father if mankind makes the right choice towards purity and rejection of corrupt patterns of the modern world.

HOW TO ACHIEVE PEACE

Unshakeable peace. Nervousness, as a consequence of the adaptive remodeling, is opposite to it. Spiritual people have to remain in a state of elevated voiceless prayer for at least 2-3 hours a day, which brings to external (1), inner (2), blissful (3) and eternal (4) peace.

Perfect ones have to achieve the fourth stage of eternal peace through unworldly, uplifting meditative prayer.

Do not puzzle out the ephemeral. Remain indifferent to it, in the same way as people of this world are indifferent to spirituality.

I embrace my disciples with my heart and achieve peace together with them, otherwise the fruits of the spiritual path would be insignificant, no matter how great the spiritual teaching is.

ABOUT ABLUTIONS

Do ablutions in holy springs more often. For most people, do it once a week. For beginners – several times a day, in order to wash off the poisonous dust that sticks to the subtle body.

ABOUT THE END TIMES

You are living in times of great spiritual discord. Keep to the fathers' path, do not abandon repentance and the last truth, conscientious prayer and life by faith, no matter what the circumstances are; be fearless, and do not let the cross slip out of your hands and God will bless you and crown you, unworthy, showing miracles of His mercy.

Time flies several times faster now, and the punishment for sinfulness and unwillingness to repent comes sooner than ever before.

The state of the world is disastrous, and God chooses more radical means: the Woman Clothed with the Sun has been sent to the world. Do the dozens and hundreds of Her apparitions all over the world not convince of the greatness of the Queen of Heaven's mission? Why are churches in a sleep? Why do the priests fight against the Divine Mother?

Repent! Disasters are close! Read the signs in the sky. The earth is on the verge of death. Keep watch vigilantly. Pray for lost souls, for the aborted, for women who had an abortion, for single mothers and abandoned children. Day and night millions cry out to heaven: 'Who will pray for us, dear mother, if not you? Who will take care of us? Where is the patronage and prayer of the church?'

The world will be plunged into the atmosphere of another existence: the descending of new energies on the earth, both divine and infernal. The saints will descend surrounded by this modified atmosphere and different breath of existence, and abide among the living. In the new order of life it will be easier to perceive the saints.

Christ Himself in glory and the Woman Clothed with the Sun will lead the descent of the saints: they will wear a solar attire with crowns on their heads. A triumphant procession of saints, an assembly of angels and righteous virgins, a constellation of elders, a council of martyrs and a council of teachers of the true Church of Christ (there will be twelve lesser councils in this great council) will follow them.

New light will come upon the earth, embrace and transform everything. Wherever the saints appear, it will be their victory and the panic flight of the devil.

Those who will not accept the Revelation about the end times, will bitterly mourn when these times come.

LOVE FOR PEOPLE

In order to pray for peace and for the conversion of sinners, one must love people.

Bow when meeting each other as if you see a living icon in front of you and the image of God, which is imprinted and crucified within the near one.

The main sin against purity of the heart is judgement or

seeing bad sides in your neighbour. Beware of this sin, and do not speak of anyone with prejudice.

PATRONESS IN THE CATHAR COMMUNITIES

Tell my Spanish children: I am their mother and patroness in the Cathar communities.

The Cathar mothers of San Salvador Verdadero have received me with great joy and initiated into the highest mysteries, saying: 'You are the second elder of Holy Spain, after John Bogomil. Father John has revealed Catharism to the world and you open to mankind our holy Cathar spiritual path, mysteries of the practical metanoia and transformation, which we have been keeping only for chosen souls.'

Also tell my Spanish children to be more zealous on the path of unworldliness, to break with the order of this world resolutely, regardless of what it would promise them, and to imprint on their brow the statutes of our Most High Father.

*

The Mother of God endowed me with the gift of managing the fates of souls and I, my child, in order to console you for your endevours as a messenger, will send you assistants and thousands of disciples. Remember one thing: your cross will multiply. You then endure, as I endured in my earthly days.

ABOUT MOZART AND THE LYRE OF ORPHEUS

I asked about Mozart.

Mozart... I saw him among heavenly assemblies. He was immediately adorned with the crown for his martyrdom.

What music does he write to the Divine Father! Mozart's heavenly operas are sung by the minstrels of the celestial cities. Mozart resides in the same destiny as other slandered saints. He would like to write an opera on your 'Euphrosinia's Psalter'.

You, my child, have been poisoned and slandered and will one day find yourself in the same destiny as Mozart, whose pieces you perform so often.

Sacred objects related to the Holy Grail.
Photo: Makariy Parfionov

Celestial beings listen with delight to your performances of musical opuses and wonder: 'Is anything like this possible on the earth? When Father John plays Mozart's piano concerts, sonatas and symphonies, he achieves the stage of a celestial minstrel. How is that possible?!'

Heaven unites with Earth, when the Lyre of Orheus is in the hands of the anointed one.

PROSTRATIONS WITH MOTHER EUPHROSINIA

Let peace be in you hearts.

I am forever with you in my prayers and especially with those who do prostrations at night in spite of any opposing or oppressive circumstances.

Fly while doing prostrations with me. When I ascended to the Kingdom, I did not stop doing prostrations, but on the contrary, multiplied them! The only difference is that it is a million times easier to do prostrations in heavens and just after three prostrations you are elevated to the throne of our Kind Father and his chariot of millions of kind eyes.

Some other strangers knock for a long time... Then suddenly the gates open and they can observe the well-organized Kingdom of ineffable kindness, wisdom, love, peace and purity, but then, alas!, the gates close. And it takes very long before they open again, while souls pass their cleansing ordeals. How hard do they mourn then!

For you, the gates will open and will never close...

Peace! Peace and grace to mankind. •

“

WITH THE DEPARTURE OF EVERY SAINT, THE HOLY GIFTS ONLY MULTIPLY ON THE EARTH. OF COURSE, THE FLOCK GRIEVES THAT THE GREAT LUMINARY HAS PASSED AWAY... HOWEVER, HIS GRACE INCREASES PROPORTIONALLY TO HIS SPIRITUAL GROWTH IN HEAVEN AND THEN SPREADS ALL OVER THE WORLD. HIS FLOCK BECOMES WORLDWIDE.

”

JOHN BOGOMIL

THE TREASURE OF FOUR INCARNATIONS

MYSTERIES OF OTHERWORLDLY PATHS FOR IMMORTAL SOULS

Where do souls go post mortem? What kind of trial do they undergo? Nothing is clear... Christians' and Jews' explanations are nebulous. Cathars believed that these religions knew nothing about God or about man and believed that their understanding of the soul's journey in the beyond, was mistaken. Belief in the Last Judgement and the tortures of the damned is total speculation and the fruit of a pathological imagination of inquisitors. May heaven keep us from approaching the shrine of the Roman Dragon with their heretical teachings!

The Hindu idea of karma and metempsychosis was also familiar to Cathars and was seen as cold-hearted or Luciferian. There is no love in it, only a blind law acts. There is no Divine Wisdom, Solar Cross or Holy Grail. This is still a version of Judeo-Christian teaching in the interpretation of Eastern mysticism.

CATHARISM IS BASED ON HEAVENLY LOVE, MINNE, WHICH IS CONCEALED FROM THE WORLD, BUT CONSIDERED BY THE CATHARS TO BE UNIQUE AND ABOVE ALL.

THE ONLY GOAL OF HUMAN LIFE IS TO OPEN THE FATHER'S LOVE ON THE EARTH MORE THAN IN HEAVEN, IN SPITE OF THE SEVERE AND PARADOXICAL CONDITIONS MANKIND HAS TO FACE.

MERCIFUL INCARNATIONS

The doctrine of a single incarnation looks silly in front of eternity. Cathars teach about *four types of incarnations.*

The elixir of immortality is not given to any agrippas or fausts or mephistopheles. Realizing that a soul is not able to remain on the earth forever, the prince of this world would like to keep it for himself and pull it into his cosmic nets and virtual traps of mammon and lust.

The first trap, which means to captivate souls from heaven into the trap of the material world, is not enough for the Evil One. He tries to stretch out his cosmic nets. That is why he invented his institutions in the afterlife: hell and paradise, purgatory and inferno, staircase of severe trials and eternal tortures... He drags a soul from disaster to disaster, from one black hole to another. And at last, when he finally swindles and weakens it, he requires renunciation of itself (!), which means the second death.

First the soul had renounced the Father and came to the devil. And then it is forced to renounce itself being entrapped in the Evil One's nets, in his Auschwitz-like astral camps of death...

However, it is all fake. The true reality and existence belong to the Divine Father and His Great Church of love. The world is managed by the Holy Grail, i.e. the inner sacred Chalice of pure, perfect and anointed ones...

THE GODDESS VIRGIN MOTHER RULES OVER THE COSMOS (HIGHER AND LOWER). EVEN THE FOURTH (ASTRAL) DIMENSION IS SECRETLY PREVAILED BY OUR MOST HIGH, WHOSE LANGUAGE IS MERCY. DIVINE WISDOM ASSIGNED SEVERAL MERCIFUL INCARNATIONS TO EVERY SOUL.

1. CATASTROPHE

The hypnotism of the Evil One should be rejected at once. He says that 'it is better for a soul to be on the earth', allegedly its ceaseless potential will be released here, which has been deliberately sealed by the Divinity in heaven...

The first incarnation of the soul on the earth is a catastrophe. It often ends as a life catastrophe, which means diseases, anxieties, death... and other endless fatal trials.

The soul, wishing to break into 'the superior existence', fell down and crashed. It ended shattered.

The basic earthly state of a soul is a shock. It experiences horror, fears and paranoia. It is driven crazy, traumatised and attacked by evil thoughts. It tries to escape from itself, longs to fulfill unrealisable desires and life goals. Finally, it loses its bearings and faces global deceit of this world...

– For what reason have I come here? I cannot understand anything. It seems there is no way out, and it is no longer possible to stay here either. Is a suicide the last resort? No, it is not the best means, but to continue to live this way is impossible...

Such is a minor crisis...

Many souls experience an intuitive horror when approaching the earth, and they do not want to incarnate. Some are happy to be aborted or mutilated still in the mother's womb, to withdraw from the earth as far as possible.

The post-mortem state of a soul after each of the incarnations is defined by Cathars as preparation. The minor otherworldly Consolamentum of the soul consists in its consolation and forgiveness; then comes insight and discernment of good and evil; assisted by the elder, a soul spiritually analyses its earthly life and passes through re-introspection; the next stage of Consolamentum includes spiritual ablution, purification, and, finally, the realization that the correct choice should be made.

The soul yearns to be changed. Oh, in its new life it will act differently! It sees its mistakes. It will not fall into the Evil One's nets anymore. It will be able to defeat him!

The soul craves for the flight again... And Divine Wisdom allows it to bruise itself against the earth like a bird before it builds its eternal nest.

2. INTRODUCTION TO THE HOLY GRAIL

In the *second incarnation* the personal, family, national and universal programs of a soul start anew.

The second incarnation is always easier and more bearable than the first. The soul is purer and its chalice of sins is not so heavy. It is not easy to lure it into traps and deceptions. It does not stay in 'town pubs' (temptations of this world) for too long and it serves the prince of darkness much less than before. It does not yield to temptations of lust, seeks to run away from evil and withdraws into itself. Then it begins to read, study and think. Animal instinct pleasures are replaced with reasonable reflection, and rationality with a mystical illumination.

The *deep crisis of the second incarnation* comes next. The soul is completely disappointed in all earthly pleasures. There is no rest, no peace, and no interest for it. Its ideals have not come true.

Complete disenchantment comes after: in career, family, politics, state service or service to the near ones...

The soul understands that *on Earth it is not possible to compensate the loss of heaven*. And it begins to feel endlessly nostalgic for celestial settlements and castles.

After a deep crisis, having happily avoided Rex Mundi's traps (this is one of the temptations within the second incarnation), already in its mature years, or in the decline of the second incarnation, a person often succeeds to find the true path. No matter how clandestine or tabooed by the prince of this world, and even sealed it would be.

The person can feel the support of deities and saints, who pray for chosen souls. Inquiring the truth, the soul approaches its minor Consolamentum.

A DAO OF MINOR CONSOLAMENTUM

Who fulfills it? How is it done? It happens inexplicably. The minor Consolamentum can be obtained from the hands of an ordinary nurse in the concentration camp's barrack or from an aid-man on the battlefield or even from a dog's tongue that licked the wound of a dying man at the accident site...

Such is the first consolation, called 'a minor Consolamentum'. Such is the *introduction to the Grail*, which is the great mystery of Earth.

The soul finally succeeds to find the divine purports, even though they would be revealed to it several seconds before leaving for eternity. A dazzling light shows the mystery of the Earth, which is union with the Most-High through passing *strastnoye* (dedicated blissful suffering).

WHILE BEING ON EARTH IN STRASTNOYE, A PERSON CAN PRODUCE MYRRHIC OILS WHICH DO NOT EXIST EVEN IN THE ANGELIC WORLDS. THESE OILS ARE PRICELESS.

When the soul returns to heaven, it bears in its heart a small vessel with myrrh. It is the fruit of earthly strastnoye. The soul brings this vessel to the Divine Wisdom as a sign of its gratitude, and, with a heavy sigh, rests on the arms of the Heavenly Lady.
The second incarnation is over. Oh, how tired is the soul! It would never come to the earth again, though it loves its neighbours infinitely and grieves about parting with them...

When Wisdom opens to the soul the inmost recesses of the Most High's love, the deepest sorrow begins...

In the first incarnation, a soul starts to repent deeply. During the second incarnation, it sheds endless tears and cries tenderly. There is no end for the soul's gratitudes. It sees the infinite mercy of the Father and wishes to thank Him, who luckily freed it from the earthly fetter!

Love starts to flame up, and Divine Wisdom inserts an ever-burning candle in the heart. The soul utters: 'I am thirsty! Oh, I long to come to this world again to help my Father and Mother to free souls from their sufferings! Oh, my Goodness, how much do they suffer (celestials are able to see the joint suffering of mankind)! No, no! How can I watch indifferently my dear brothers and sisters, my children suffering in the devil's nets?'

Filled with righteous desire to help them, the soul asks the Most-High to let it return into the world. And then Divine Wisdom does not allow either first or second incarnation, but blesses the soul to come to Earth in *the third incarnation*, which is pure.

3. THE FEAT OF LOVE AND SACRIFICE

The first two incarnations are tempting. The third and fourth are redemptive.

On arrival to the world for the third time the soul is seized with higher metaphysical impulses. It overcomes meanness, narrow-mindedness, double-dealing and mercenariness. It is seeking the sublime, light and eternal.

The soul as a disciple of the Most High is not content with anything mundane any more. It is seeking to implement the ideal of the Father, i.e. to live on Earth according to celestial laws and acquire *pure love*. It becomes reconciled with itself, God, the world and changes its inner principles. The soul makes many efforts to transform completely and often looks into the 'inner casket', wondering if its compositions have changed from serpentine to divine.

The third incarnation is expiatory. The soul is full of desire to perform the heroic deeds of love and self-sacrifice with the purpose to thank the Father as much as it can.

The power of metaphysical spiritual experience allows the soul to convince many people to easily follow the true teacher, the anointed one, not to be afraid of the aggressive institutions of the prince of this world and to be ready to die for love of its neighbour... It is deeply convinced of eternal life and is strong in faith. Sin loses all power over such a soul. It joins the host of the Most High, and is clothed with the immaculate garment of the Goddess Virgin Mother. It is honoured with the crown of the victor. The Holy Grail is in front of its gaze. It holds a spear or a sword in its right hand, a shield in the left, and rides the white horse of the spiritual knighthood.

Having offered a self-sacrifice and carried its cross, the soul, passing through suffering, spiritual challenges and anointings, ascends step-by-step to the throne of Divine Wisdom... However, there it grieves even more.

How insignificant were its attempts to help the Most High! How much evil there is still in the world, how much hypnosis and slander! How painful it is for our Father and how much does He suffer!

The soul starts to long even stronger and the candle of Heavenly Love is lit in the heart. It now yearns for more than peace - for the matrimony with the Divinity through suffering mankind (!).

Then Divine Wisdom gives the soul a kiss of love and sends it into the world.

4. THE SOARING FLIGHT OF THE WHITE EAGLE

The fourth incarnation is the soaring flight of the white eagle: the glorious embodiment of the Perfect (Parfait) or chalice-bearer (royal guardian of the Holy Grail).

The faith of the first incarnation is blind and instinctive. In the second incarnation, seeking to become free from the magnets of the world, souls get caught in a new trap, which is the institutional church (a known hypocrite, pretending to be a servant of God while it serves the prince of darkness, the great tempter). Only at the end of the second incarnation, when the soul is given the honour of receiving the minor Consolamentum (e.g., an Orthodox elder begins to see clearly the shocking truth about the institutional church to which he belonged), it looks for initiation into the Heavenly Church. The third incarnation presupposes a full Cathar Consolamentum and victory over both traps: (1) worldly and (2) religious...

Only in the fourth incarnation, the soul achieves the third stage of Consolamentum (what Mother Euphrosinia called the highest stage of acquisition of the All-Holy Spirit). The Spirit-Bridegroom more than embraces the soul-bride, He calls it His divine wife. And the Perfect becomes a minor Christ (anointed one) and participates in eternal co-redemption.

The further ways of the soul are mysterious. The Cathars preferred not to speak about them, referring to the origin of Divine Wisdom, to the Holy Grail...

The scheme shown above reveals a plan of Divine Wisdom and the Most High, which reflects a realistic path of a soul in the most merciful way. However, schemes can be deviated from. The soul can abandon coming into the world while on the way down or it can master three incarnations in one life (via great breakthroughs and trials). It may go through more than two tempting incarnations and more than two redemptive ones...

There are souls 'from beneath' that do not come to experience the love of the Father but for the sake of increasing in evil. The Evil One gives them his damned 'consolations' and abominable initiations. Some souls fall down from fatal otherworldly trajectories onto the earth and shatter...

There are other stages 'before' and 'after' the listed above. Black incarnations 'from beneath' are before listed, incarnations 'from above' are after. Then the fifth, sixth stages, and up to the eighth, which is related to the union with the Most High and embodiment in other mystical bodies.

At every stage the vision of the Father's face astonishes the soul with the revelation of infinite kindness. He is kinder and kinder each time. Whatever may happen to the soul, whatever traps it may fall into, no matter how many mistakes it can make, the Most High gives it His love and wisdom more and more. And He apportions suffering so mercifully that it turns to the soul with multiplied beatitudes.

Everywhere is only the glory and love of our Most High! The soul starts to see His love not due to neurotic shocking states of fear, despair or endless tears, but experiences it peacefully and blissfully. Having experienced this love, the soul takes the vow (first of all to itself!) not to repeat the mistakes and never betray the kindest Father. •

The pearl icon of the III millennium. Beadwork of Nikolina Kravchenko.

THERE ARE BOOKS THAT ARE BORN AND DIE AS SOON AS THE LAST READER READS THEM. BUT 'DON QUIXOTE', BASED ON ARCHETYPES, WAS CROWNED WITH IMMORTALITY AND BECAME AN ETERNAL SCROLL.

MARIO DE GRACIA, VICTORIA BONMATI

SPAIN

THE KNIGHT OF HEAVENLY COUNTENANCE

'I am no longer Don Quixote of La Mancha, but Alonso Quixano the kind one.....' [23]

These are the last words with which the Knight of the Sad Countenance bade farewell to this world. This is living proof that there is no higher ideal than to come to our deathbed as KIND, a million times kinder... the kindest of the kind!!

He was not mad. He was just *kind*.

> *'My intentions are always directed to worthy ends, to do good to all and evil to none; and if he who means this, does this, and makes this his practice, he deserves to be called a fool, it is for your highnesses to say...'*

Herein lies the secret of the world-wide success of the work of Miguel de Cervantes Saavedra, as the *story of Don Quixote implies the mystery of a man's arrival to earth*. These are archetypal pearls threaded on one of the most beautiful among written stories!

1. ALONSO QUIXANO AS EARTHLY HEAVENLY-DWELLER

A human being comes into this world full of threatening mills (pillars of evil), and as an errant knight, fearless and guided from above, winning in all battles, till the last one, in the name of good.

Don Quixote personified a soul of universal scale that takes the spear of truth fearlessly and fights up to its last breath in order to win a victory over thousands of manifestations of global evil, such as usurpation and lies, inversion and selfishness... But his real virtue is rooted in the *absolute altruism of a heroic deed*, which is not made for acquiring personal glory.

WINNING FOR ONE'S OWN SAKE MEANS NOTHING. VICTORIES GAINED WITH A SIMILAR MOTIVATION, DIE WITH MAN ON HIS DEATHBED... CERVANTES SPEAKS ABOUT A MUCH MORE PROFOUND AND SUBLIME PURPOSE:
TO CONQUER IN THE NAME OF HUMANITY, AND TO LEAVE THE WORLD BEHIND AFTER MAKING IT BETTER, OR TO TESTIFY THAT ONLY GOOD PEOPLE REMAIN IN ONE'S MEMORY.

2. SANCHO PANZA AS A FAITHFUL BROTHER

One of the greatest mysteries of the work, *brotherhood*, lies in the tender image of Sancho.

The bond between Don Quixote and Sancho Panza went beyond the limits of the formal statute that should be expected in the relationship between a squire and his master. Don Quixote and Sancho united their lives,

23
From the book 'Don Quixote of La Mancha' by Miguel de Cervantes. Translated by John Ormsby.

having the noblest aim. Despite all the outward differences between them, they succeeded to establish a union, which was based only on a pure, innocent and faithful love till the end.

Love transformed them. The knight and his squire became brothers, adoring each other in spite of all. Each of them put his heart as a living shield and was not afraid to die, as they *already* had given their lives for love... They were inseparable, these sworn brothers, and became one.

> *'... Mine (master)... has nothing of a rogue in him, - Sancho said about Don Quixote.- He has the soul of a pitcher; he has no thought of doing harm to anyone..., and for this simplicity I love him as I love the core of my heart, and I can't bring myself to leave him, no matter how many foolish things he does.'*

Don Quixote could not do without Sancho either. Their strength arose from their brotherhood and boundless love, which is manifested by two souls in a divine union with each other and with all humanity...

Despite the fact that Sancho confessed himself to be a simple uncouth servant, he possessed innate wisdom:

> *'Let us leave it all to God', he says to his dearest master; 'who alone knows what is to happen in this vale of tears, in this evil world of ours, where there is hardly a thing to be found without some mixture of wickedness, roguery, and rascality'.*

3. DULCINEA AS THE HEAVENLY LADY

> *'Recollect, Sancho,' replied Don Quixote, 'there are two sorts of beauty, one of the mind, the other of the body; that of the mind displays and exhibits itself in intelligence, in modesty, in honourable conduct, in generosity, in good breeding; and all these qualities are possible and may exist in an ugly man; and when it is this sort of beauty and not that of the body that is the attraction, love is apt to spring up suddenly and violently'.*

Cervantes would like to show virginal love to the most beautiful woman in the world. Was Dulcinea del Toboso not the personification of the Heavenly Mother, Who accompanies mysteriously every step of Her knight? She is a source of inspiration and nourishing from above indeed, the Guide Who unconditionally protects and truly defeats in every battle. The Heavenly Queen is the only sword and shield of Don Quixote:

> *'... the might of Dulcinea employed my arm as the instrument of her achievements... She fights in me and conquers in me, and I live and breathe in her, and owe my life and being to her.'*

DULCINEA (TRANSLATED AS THE SWEETEST) IS THE MAIN CHARACTER OF THE WORK. ONLY THE HEAVENLY LADY IS A CENTRAL AXIS OF THE MINISTRY AND THE VERY LIFE OF EVERY KNIGHT. VICTORY IS IMPOSSIBLE WITHOUT HER AS GUIDE.

One day Don Quixote delayed merchants on the road and demanded loudly that they should confirm that Dulcinea del Toboso was more beautiful than all women on earth. They refused, referring to the fact that they had never seen her... This is a trivial argumentation of this world.

> *'If I were to show her to you,' replied Don Quixote, 'what merit would you have in confessing a truth so manifest? The essential point is that without seeing her you must believe, confess, affirm, swear, and defend it...'*

Miguel de Cervantes was not a utopian dreamer who imagines a better world. He knew in practice the statutes of superior good, learned the rules of spiritual battle. The weapons of the knight's victory are mercy, loyalty, courage and following the last truth... And the most important is allegiance to the White Lady, the immaculate Mother and Bride. Without devotion to Her one is able to achieve nothing.

> *'For to deprive a knight-errant of his lady is to deprive him of the eyes he sees with, of the sun that gives him light.... An errant knight without a lady is like a tree without leaves, a building without a foundation, or a shadow without the body that causes it.'*

4. THE MILLS AS THE GREAT MECHANISM OF WORLD EVIL

The mills appear not only in the famous passage that is known to all, even to those who have not read the novel.

They are scattered about the book, reflecting *thousands of masks that hide evil*. However, Cervantes shows them openly as cement pillars of the great mechanism of world evil that suppresses and forbids the flowering of kindness:

> *'We have to slay pride in giants, envy by generosity and nobleness of heart, anger by calmness of demeanour and equanimity, gluttony and sloth by our frugality and the length of our vigils, lust and lewdness by loyalty, ...indolence by crossing the world in all directions seeking opportunities of making ourselves, besides Christians, famous knights.'*

DON QUIXOTE REALIZED THAT IT IS NOT NECESSARY TO FIGHT AGAINST THE EXTERNAL MANIFESTATIONS OF EVIL, BUT TO UNDERCUT ITS VERY ROOT, WHICH HAS ALWAYS BEEN THE SOURCE OF ALL MISFORTUNES... IT IS USELESS TO TRY TO SHIELD FROM THE ARROWS SHOT AT THE KNIGHT, IF HE DOES NOT KNOW WHO THE ARCHER IS.

5. 'IT'S THE CHURCH WE HAVE COME UPON, SANCHO.' RELIGIOUS TRAP

Throughout the novel Don Quixote conflicts with the priests, describing them as thieves, sly and crafty scoundrels. In the servants of the Roman Church the great Cathar bard Cervantes exposes the traps of this world and the sorcerers which mesmerize souls with their black tricks in order to manipulate them.

> *'...God bless me!' said the duke aloud at this, 'who can have done the world such an injury? Who can have robbed it of the beauty that gladdened it?..'*
>
> *'Who?' replied Don Quixote; 'who could it be but some malignant enchanter of the many that persecute me out of envy—that accursed race born into the world to obscure and bring to naught the achievements of the good, and glorify and exalt the deeds of the wicked?...'*

This is an originally Cathar thesis, reminiscent of the angry words of the evangelical Christ to the pharisees of all times!

Don Quixote and Sancho Panza. Illustration by Gustave Dore

KNIGHTS OF GOOD AND VIRGINITY

How much required in our modern world —with its continuing armed conflicts, that threaten to go into a world war—, are such noble knights in the highest sense, of heavenly image, whose standard is peace!

> “ *'The purpose and limit of the aspirations of [martial arts] is peace, and peace is the highest of all earthly goods'.*

Knights of good are alive. They never disappeared. Were Buddha and Zoroaster, Christ and Francis of Assisi, St. Sergius of Radonezh and Seraphim of Sarov not knights of superior kindness? Did Seraphim the Tender not commit chivalrous deeds of kindness on Solovki? And is blessed John Bogomil not the Cervantes and Don Quixote of the 21st century?

He is Don Quixote as far as he has already put on the armour and has taken his shield and spear out onto the battlefield. He is Cervantes as long as he is holding the pen of the All-Highest, which describes the fate of the new knights guided by the Most Pure.

'ANOTHER QUIXOTE': THE BOGOMIL KNIGHTHOOD OF THE CALIPHATE OF CORDOBA

How did Cervantes get this treasure of wisdom? Who gave him the mystery of the knight archetype?

The answer can seem paradoxical: the *Arab Bogomils.*

Since childhood, Miguel tried to live according to the highest ideals and sought knight feats. At the age of 10 he entered the Jesuits Order College, but being disappointed with lies and hypocrisy reigning there, he ran away in order to join the army and be closer to the true hidalgos. It was then that the image of a knight of noble countenance became his ideal, and his first poems were born.

In 1575, Cervantes, after a series of military campaigns (including the Battle of Lepanto, which gave him the famous nickname of 'One-armed man of Lepanto') sat on the galley 'Sun' for returning to Spain. However, off the coast of Catalonia, the ship was boarded by the Turkish corsairs. This event had a profound effect on Miguel, who lived in captivity by the Algerian Berbers for five years.

Captivity became for him a yurodivy way of knowledge of the mysteries, it formed the basis for his work. It was in captivity when he read the Arabic manuscript of 'another Quixote[24].'

The mentioned manuscript was most likely one of the legends of the *Caliphate of Cordoba.*

24
Cervantes's mention of the 'Arab historian Sid Hamete Benengeli', whose book about Don Quixote he allegedly had read in Toledo, can serve as an indirect evidence of this.

RELIGIONS ARE TRANSIENT. KNIGHTHOOD IS ETERNAL

The Caliphate of Cordoba, which was believed to be the centre of Islamic civilization in the 9th –10th centuries, was a unique *case of a Temple of Peace.* Under the authority of the righteous emirs and caliphs of Cordoba lived: the kind Christian-Bogomils, who had taken refuge from Byzantine persecutions, the good Jews of Babylon mark (the Babylonian 'doves'), who had renounced the mixed Torah of the Maccabees, and the good Muslims who preached the original Islam.

The *worship of the Queen of Peace and the Most Merciful Mother* was common to all of them. Peace comes immediately, all frictions are resolved, black holes are sealed and fly droppings in the inner are removed at the mention of Her name.

At the court of the caliph Abd ar-Rahman III served the Slavic knights-sakalibas, who were the descendants of the Scythian warriors-knights and bearers of the spirituality of the Nightingale Mountain Grail, having been devoted to the sweetest Virgin. Their secret statutes might form the basis of the legend, which fell into the hands of the captive Spaniard.

Gripped with its story, Cervantes began to see clearly that knighthood knows no national identity! It is in the universum of all world cultures. The noble Visigoth-paladins and Sufi *dzhovanmardins* (literally 'young heroes-bogatyrs'), the Berber horsemen of Hannibal and the warriors-poets of Cordoba and Granada Caliphates were knights of heavenly countenance...

The purpose of knighthood is to defeat world evil. But first it is necessary to win it inside.

Yes, evil is outside,
but first evil is inside me.

Cervantes concludes that *religions are transient. Knighthood* (which is seemingly historically conditional) *is eternal.*

A man, especially a young man, is called to become a knight of light against the forces of world evil, madmen and destroyers of the world, which make believe they are saviours. Only the knights of the last truth can stop their maniacal madness. Protection of our heavenly Lady to them, whatever faith they may profess!

THE GREATEST GENIUS OF SPAIN KNEW HIS SOLOVKI

Cervantes was a prisoner a few more times, but imprisonment did not close his ardent heart. On the contrary, he became wiser and kinder. In prison he felt free, but at large... he seemed a convict.

Spain gave Miguel an unkind reception. Having scented a bearer of a different spirituality, the prince of this world put him to blows and test, followed by years of poverty, slander and imprisonment... The devoted knight was born in persecutions.

Cervantes wrote his 'Don Quixote' in his prison cell, allegorically remembering what he had been tutored by the Bogomil spiritual heroes. No walls or barbed wires can limit the blissful ministry. The greatest genius of Spain reached the height of the spiritual path, having known his own Solovki....

The image of Don Quixote de la Mancha, which became revolutionary in its time, has been and will continue to be such until good wins the final victory over evil! This book will not disappear with the debris of this world, '*which has its own appointed end*' as far as its character is eternal. The immortal scrolls exist not only in the libraries of this world, but are imprinted in the most splendid and highest intergalactic and eternal Mystical library of thousands of good worlds.

While the sacred battle is in progress on Earth, 'The Ingenious Gentleman Don Quixote of La Mancha' will be a living book, capable to awaken the knight of good and virginity enclosed in every soul! •

Miguel de Cervantes Saavedra. ►
Engraving, 1870.

MIKHAIL STEPANENKO: 'HUMANITY NEEDS MUSICAL PROPHETS!'

IT IS TIME TO RETURN THE MUSIC INTO THE REALM OF A PRAYER

Int.: It is known that when the Divine Mother appears to modern visionaries, often the most beautiful music is heard, which cannot be described by any words. Do you believe in the reality of a musical revelation?

Music is a primary existence. In the beginning, the Music started with sound, and then it turned into the Word. The concept of Pythagoras's 'music of the heavenly spheres' (macrocosm) describes heavenly music which has then come to the earth.

Do you know that the person who had devised the names of musical notes, an Italian Guido d'Arezzo (11th century), used the first syllables of a spiritual hymn? Do from '*DOminus*' (the Lord), re from '*REsonare fibris*' (the soul's strings began to sound) etc. The scales arose from a higher state of mind, or prayer! Now it is time to return the music into the realm of a prayer.

When Mozart was writing his music (as we know, he had been doing it since he was four years old), he always received a revelation. A melody was born within him, and at the same time it was the divine music. Mozart confronted Roman pharisaism with his spiritual genius!

Mozart, Tchaikovsky, Beethoven... gained the union with that One who was out-of-reach. They entered the spheres inaccessible for other musicians. Herein is the greatness of their music. Communication at such high level helps to look at yourself adequately and to assess the state of your own heart sensibly.

Epochs pass and musical styles change depending on the personality of the composer... The main thing remains permanent – the aspiration to an ideal, which is the Divinity.

Int.: It seems that the lack of aspiration for the Divinity prevents from perceiving the music up to the mark. A soul becomes like the pig under an oak from the famous fable. A Russian media person (by the way, he is a priest!) has recently claimed: 'Mozart composed monotonous and pop pieces'.

M.S.: The spiritual condition of a society depends on what kind of ideals prevail and what images are imposed on people. From birth, man has great talents, which he should seek to reveal completely. However, most people suppress their latent talents themselves, if they, for instance, watch TV.

Modern mass media dupe their customers. They clog up the brains with unnecessary information in order to block the person's mind and soul and ultimately plunge him into a pit, so that he is not able to get out from it. It is always easier to come down, as there is no need to make efforts. In order to ascend, you have to make efforts.

Music has a great purpose: *it helps to ascend*. The great musicians such as Tchaikovsky endeavored to get into the spheres of harmony, purity and beauty. Therefore, their music directs the listeners up the ladder of perfection, into the spheres of celestial harmony.

TO TEACH THE MUSIC MEANS TO TRAIN THE SOUL

Int.: Many people today are concerned about self-improvement. However their understanding of this process is very limited; getting the second university degree or learning to play a new musical instrument, losing weight or building muscle... At best, 'to find harmony with oneself'. It is just self-perfection in the worldly order.

M.S.: Mankind needs the music of highly devoted people or 'keepers of the sphere'! Only the music of messengers from heaven will help to pull people out of the abyss which they have fallen into, and to lead them to unprecedented heights of another world, which is full of celestial harmonies.

MIKHAIL STEPANENKO is an outstanding Ukrainian composer, musician and a teacher, head of the department of special Piano of the Kiev Conservatory. An Honoured cultural worker of Ukraine and Russia, and a National artist of Ukraine. In 1992-2004 he was the head of the Ukrainian Union of composers.

Photo: Ekaterina Stepanova

I would like to be a saint... in both the oldest and the newest sense of this word. (I identify the well-known people with this word: Buddha, Epicurus and Christ, Epictetus and Francis of Assisi... not mentioning others).

If I had great talents in any field of spiritual life or activity: in philosophy, poetry, literature or one of the various kinds of art... then my secret longing for 'holiness', my dream about serving for goodness and goodness only (which I have never achieved), and about submission of all my thoughts and acts to the idea of good, it all 'would take its place', because goodness would constitute all my deeds, in the same way as 'the words of a poet are already his deeds', according the precise definition of Pushkin...

Heinrich Neuhaus, 'The Diary of the last years'

M.S.: As a teacher, I try to direct my students to the perfection in order to achieve the performance of music in the way as it was conceived by the composer.

Performances of Beethoven and other great composers should be adequate to what they created. This is the core of a performer's art. A teacher's art and hard work is to teach a student to perform music in the way, that the composer originally heard it; as Beethoven heard it with his inner hearing (when he was already deaf to the external sounds).

Everyone has a talent for music. Even if you have no gift for music-making, then there is definitely a gift for listening to the music. Man through listening to the music of great composers and musicians enters the purest celestial spheres, so that he cannot be bad. The positive transformation happens, or 'covering with the composition of goodness'.

YOU CAN TEACH A STUDENT HOW TO COMPOSE FUGUES OR HOW TO ORCHESTRATE... BUT IT IS VERY DIFFERENT TO TEACH HIM HOW TO ACHIEVE SPIRITUAL HEIGHTS. SO I CALL IT NOT 'TO TEACH MUSIC', BUT TO TRAIN THE SOUL.

SCALES OF LOVE

Int.: Does not it seem to you that the soul is leaving the music? Today, in China, Japan, the USA and Europe musical performance turned into robotic virtuosity and sophisticated preoccupation with technical aspects of music-making. They do not think about the spiritual content at all!

M.S.: The majority of musicians improve their skills with the purpose to earn more money. Only some of them aim at transcendent heights of the spirit. However it should be so for everybody!

All has love in its origin. Nothing can exist without love. Love is a great motive power to the sublime. It gives a desire for perfection, transformation and further development.

The Russian philosopher, Vladimir Solovyov, said: 'Only the sun of love is motionless'. You may call John Bogomil's books and musical performances a revelation of love. The music is a perfect way to express love. It penetrates deeply into the soul and gives rise to an entire spectrum of cordial vibrations: a boy is walking around the city and hears great music taken by a composer from the higher worlds; this music touches his archetypal strings and gives birth to love within his heart.

Music school education teaches how to play common musical scales, but not the scales of love and harmony.

Int.: Our friend, a Professor of the History of Music, Evgeniy Levashev, once said, 'the trouble of many musicians is that they seek self-expression. However, the opposite is required, i.e. self-denial in the name of the Divine. Any labour could be spiritual: from cleaning latrines in the army to composing great symphonies. Everything we do should be treated as a good deed towards our dear ones.'

M.S.: Most people consider their life as a kind of business - to draw interest from investments: 'If I pray, I will attain eternal life'... This is a merely pragmatic idea. *Only 'the door of love' leads into eternal life.*

Every man has a certain mission from God, which is always extremely difficult to accomplish. In order

to fulfill this task, it is necessary to overcome oneself, i.e. not to do what is pleasant to you, but what you are supposed to do. If there are no obstacles, a person turns into a 'vegetable': he feels fine as it is.

THE MYSTICAL EXPERIENCE OF UNITY

Int.: That is why 'the keepers of the sphere' are needed; those who have entered the realm of heavenly love and dare to awaken others, to encourage them to move up, and do not stay in the 'vegetable' condition.

M.S.: I would say outright: *what does not carry love has no right to exist!* People need love. Love is both the means and the goal at the same time.

The music of great composers fosters spiritual love. Only that one can perform it appropriately, who is full of love, i.e. he has experienced it, let it pass through himself and appreciated it with all his soul.

A distinguished Russian philologist and philosopher, Sergei Averintsev, spoke about the Temple of Sophia, the Divine Wisdom. The wisdom, unfortunately, is given not to everyone. However, it can be adopted through communication with those who possess wisdom.

Next to Mozart, Beethoven and Tchaikovsky were people who could not compose music, but they were like-minded to great composers and had the same ideals. Communication with spiritual people leaves an indelible imprint as they overflow into you.

When there is love between you, *then the mystical kinship starts, i.e. the mystical experience of unity.* These notions are so high that I am even afraid to touch upon them. That what is ineffable cannot be expressed in words. As the poet Fyodor Tyutchev said: 'A thought once uttered is untrue.'

RELIGIOUSNESS AND MYSTICISM ARE MUTUALLY EXCLUSIVE CONCEPTS!

Int.: John Bogomil in his musical diary-book 'The Piano as the Lyre of Orpheus' says that playing music is inconceivable without spiritual practice, chastity and love. A musician is the messenger. His inner state should correspond to the greatness of the music he plays.

M.S.: This view is close to me. Why are we respectful to a hermit? He withdraws from the world to enter the spiritual world; tries to better understand his union with God and enter a trustful dialogue with Him. It is closely connected with mysticism.

Mysticism is a unique phenomenon that relates to your own hopes and disillusionments, spiritual battles and crises... It is impossible to refer to it as a routine. Rationality excludes mysticism!

I believe that religiosity and mysticism are mutually exclusive. Religiosity is a degraded spirituality, whereas mysticism is a result of high spirituality, which presumes a direct unity of a person with the Divine. Spirituality helps to escape from the fetters of this world, break away from the earth.

It is known that H. Neuhaus at the end of his life admitted that he wanted to become a saint. Everyone wants to bear high ideals. The more good you do to people, the more it multiplies within yourself. The same is with evil. Therefore, the musicians, who bring down the music from the highest and purest spheres, are, first of all, the winners over evil!

Int.: So, musicians have to be absolutely victorious, in order to help their listeners to overcome evil as well!

M.S.: Great music fosters the soul and gives a powerful impulse to it. Music, performed by highly devoted musicians, purifies you and makes you kinder, leads to spiritual perfection and helps to open the heart, makes you compassionate, so that you become able to feel the pain of another person as your own; it reveals the inner beauty and makes you strive for harmony in everything; the very perception of music transfers to the realm of the heart, if the heart is pure.

I will never forget the reminiscence of a well-known jazz pianist. One day he was walking by the music shop and was struck with Beethoven's 'Fur Elise' which resounded outside. What he had heard astounded him deeply and turned his 'inner axis'. Thus his fascination with Beethoven's music began. *Beethoven catches souls with his music!*

Therefore, the luminaries, the anointed ones and musical prophets are so much required. They will help mankind to purify their hearts from mental delusions, for the heart to resound like a lyre! •

MUSIC SPEAKS THE LANGUAGE OF ABSOLUTE GOOD

Fragments from the book by John Bogomil 'The Crescendo of Good', 2015.

'The book 'The Piano as the Lyre of Orpheus' does not only remind about the great musical luminaries, but also excites thirst for knowledge, i.e. to learn more about the musician, his life, work, and music.

I am very glad that this book has been published and has become the common property of many people, because it brings aspiration for the divine ideals. However many books about music and musicians have been published, none of them are comparable with this book. 'The Piano as the Lyre of Orpheus' opens a unique world for the soul, the world of heavenly love, kindness, beauty and harmony.

I express my thanks to John Bogomil for the enlightenment of the great love that he brings to mankind. I wish him to access the highest divine spheres, inexhaustible creative potential and new, more intimate, friendly dialogues!'

Mikhail Stepanenko, Head of the Ukraine Union of Composers (1989- 2005), Head of the piano department of the Ukrainian National Music Academy.

SPIRITUALITY IS ABOVE ALL!

Music should be played *in the spirit and by the spirit!* Such is my advice to musical teachers.

In the spirit means away from clichés.

By the spirit means with the All-Holy Spirit!

Spirituality is above all!!! This is especially true for the archetypal geniuses who faced the issues concerning life and death. Only music can provide a solution for them.

Music meets man and accompanies him when he leaves the earth. It is no accident that the funeral service is usually accompanied by music. However, in this case great composers would not resort to the language of requiem or funeral marches (which is the most primitive one can imagine!), but to the language of *victory of higher love over death.*

*

Music includes a set of three brilliant and strong aspects: SPIRITUALITY, EXPRESSIVENESS AND ENERGY. It is especially relevant to the classic music of Mozart and Beethoven...

MUSIC IS MAGNIFICENT BECAUSE IT SPEAKS THE LANGUAGE OF ABSOLUTE GOOD.

The musical notation interpreted with divine inspiration ('from on high') excludes evil as such. Herein lies the mystery of the music. Even if there was any evil in Berlioz, Schumann (so-called 'romanticists'), it will evaporate during such an inspired performance, so that only MUSIC will remain.

When I touch the keyboard, I adhere to my favourite concept, which is *consolamentum*, or consolation.

What is music? It is a swan song of the Bridal Chamber, free from anything earthly, but imbued with ecstatic delight. The genius is the one who hears and notes down the